CHEAM

PAST & PRESENT

S A R A   G O O D W I N S

SUTTON PUBLISHING

Sutton Publishing Limited
Phoenix Mill · Thrupp · Stroud
Gloucestershire · GL5 2BU

First published 2003

Copyright © Sara Goodwins, 2003

British Library Cataloguing in Publication Data
A catalogue record for this book is available from the
British Library.

ISBN 0-7509-3423-9

Typeset in 10.5/13.5 Photina.
Typesetting and origination by
Sutton Publishing Limited.
Printed and bound in England by
J.H. Haynes & Co. Ltd, Sparkford.

Title page photograph: Cheam Road, looking east from the village centre crossroads, 21 June 2003. There has been a Harrow Inn in Cheam for about 400 years, although the current building, on the right of the photograph, was built in about 1936. About that time the road was doubled in width and many old buildings, including the old Harrow premises were demolished. The village sign was erected in 2001 to commemorate the millennium and silently perpetuates the argument about whether the millennium is correctly 2000 or 2001. The sign shows two of Cheam's best-known landmarks: Whitehall and the spire of St Dunstan's Church. (*George Hobbs*)

> *For Miss Smith.*
> *You taught me a lot:*
> *thank you.*

Cheam Road, looking east, c. 1920. Originally a turnpike road built in 1755, Cheam Road linked Carshalton to Ewell and was the first highway of any significance to pass through Cheam. This view is taken from near the crossroads at the top of the High Street, about 100 yards further east from that on the title page. The triangular sign with the legend 'Carriage Drive' marks the entrance to a house called The Quarry (see page 19). The driveway now forms the part of Quarry Park Road up to the sharp right-hand bend. (*Lilian Curd*)

CONTENTS

The back of The Old Cottage, The Broadway, 1970s. Hopefully this book will reveal some of the hidden aspects of Cheam. *(Ron Taylor, Cheam Camera Club)*

INTRODUCTION

Cheam is no stranger to change. Few places can have changed quite so much in quite so short a time as Cheam in the early part of the twentieth century. Unusually, the pace of change was quicker a century ago than it is today. North Cheam was little more than a crossroads before the rush for new housing began, while Cheam Village was largely demolished and rebuilt. Even so the development was not unplanned, the building not haphazard. Unless disturbed by a natural or man-made disaster such as landslide or war, places evolve and there is usually a link, however tenuous, with what has gone before.

Names are useful signposts to an area's previous history. There is no common now near Cheam Common Road, but there was, not so long ago. The derivation of Golf Side, next to Cuddington Golf Course, is perhaps obvious, but why was the house opposite it called The Great Halfpenny? It was apparently owned by a judge; perhaps he was also a miser. Local worthies, Messrs Peach, Northey and Antrobus are remembered in Peaches Close, Northey Avenue and Antrobus Close, but why was the house at the end of Peaches Close called Cold Blow? It's not on a hill, and the wind doesn't seem to be funnelled particularly towards it. It was said to have been built by a butcher, was used by the council during the war and then by the British Legion. It has now been turned into very nice flats, but why the name? Spring Close Lane has obviously been known as a source of water for years and maps of 1847 show two small ponds virtually under what is now Sutton by-pass. Today the Sutton and East Surrey Water Company has a small pumping station in Spring Close Lane. And does anyone know the history behind Gander Green Lane? Perhaps there was more than one green, and the lane ran near the one for geese.

Each change, each new building, each new road stands out at first, but, after a surprisingly short time, locals have trouble remembering exactly what the place looked like before. That is the value of a book of this sort. Change is not necessarily bad – it can offer growth, improvement and new opportunities – but wise people will remember their history, conserve the good, discard the bad and learn from the best. History is the foundation on which we build.

Some local landmarks have been lost, some unfortunately so, but new landmarks take their place. Cheam Court Farm was demolished and Century Cinema plus a row of shops was built in its place. Then the old cinema was demolished and replaced by a Skoda garage with offices above which were occupied by Trust House Forte. Now the garage has gone, replaced in its turn by an office building which has resurrected the name of the old cinema. The row of shops opposite were built on the site of

Repairing the Hare Wall, Onslow Avenue, 14 June 2003. Bricklayer David C. Smith is continuing the work of earlier craftsmen who, by maintaining our heritage, have ensured that it is still here for us to enjoy. *(George Hobbs)*

allotment gardens; the greengrocer there might be surprised to learn that he's continuing the tradition of supplying fresh produce on site. Century House might become the Whitehall of the twenty-sixth century or might again disappear to be replaced by yet another building of its time.

Only things which are dead don't change. One of the people who kindly helped in finding and selecting the photographs for inclusion in this book, deliberately misquoted a line from the hymn 'Abide with Me'. He said that the line should more properly be: 'change *or* decay in all around I see'. He's right. Cheam has changed. It will continue to change as our community continues to evolve. We cannot stop it, and nor should we try. We can only celebrate what has been and look forward to being part of the future.

Several memorable books with stunning photographs have already been published about Cheam, notably by Frank Burgess, and there is an excellent collection of photographic material held in the Sutton Heritage Collection by Sutton Library. This book, however, has attempted to show a side of Cheam which is perhaps less well documented, using photographs most of which have not previously been seen by the public. If the author has produced something which adds to the history books written about Cheam in the past, and provides a starting point for those which will undoubtedly be written in the future, she will have succeeded. If she has also managed to produce something entertaining along the way, so much the better.

1

The Two Communities

The back of Parkin's auction rooms, Park Road, 1970s. Once called the King's Hall Baptist Chapel, the building was constructed on what was formerly part of the garden of West Cheam Manor House. The manor house itself was situated on the site of what is now Cheam branch library. The house was demolished in 1796, but the grounds remained into the twentieth century. The supporting wall in front of the war memorial garden and bordering Malden Road, although lower than originally built, once surrounded the manor grounds and is one of the very few visible remnants of the house. Parkin's has hardly changed at all since this picture was taken. I wonder what the guard dog's dreaming about?
(Ron Taylor, Cheam Camera Club)

People have been living in Cheam for two millennia, judging by the Roman pottery found in Manor Road and the remains of a Saxon building incorporated into the Lumley chapel. But why here? Why did our ancestors decide that this particular hollow between two not very big hills would make a good site for a settlement?

Water. Water is the key. Not perhaps to the choice of this area, which would become south-west London, but certainly to the choice of this hollow. The geology of the area determined the development of Cheam from its earliest years until around the middle of the nineteenth century. North Cheam is built on London clay, while the southern extreme of Cheam Village is on chalk. Between the two is a belt of Thanet sand, on which the oldest buildings in the area are built. Thanet sand holds water which occasionally emerges as a spring, or which can be made available by digging relatively shallow wells. London clay is not very porous so moisture lingers on the surface and is easily contaminated, while water leaches through chalk as through a sieve. The railway line marks the approximate edge of the belt of Thanet sand to the south, while the northern edge corresponds roughly to a line taking in Fromondes Road.

One glance at a map reveals that most of the water-bearing soil was covered by stately homes and their grounds – which, incidentally, probably explains why some of the gardens in the area were noted for their beauty. The village was hemmed in by large properties to the east and west and by poor ground to the north and south. In the middle of the nineteenth century the only dwelling on the chalk south of Cheam Court Farm and Cheam School was Warren Cottage (see page 25) which had a well 200 feet deep. The railway may have brought additional people, but they could have nowhere to live until they could obtain a source of water. The Sutton and Cheam Water Company was incorporated on 15 June 1863, and the next four years saw Cheam Village supplied with piped water. By 1897 a good water supply was available to North Cheam. Modern Cheam had become possible.

Historically, Cheam is no stranger to being divided. In the fourteenth century there were two villages: West Cheam, a small hamlet huddled round the hill-top church and owned by the prior of the monastery attached to Canterbury Cathedral, and East Cheam, about half a mile to the east around Gander Green Lane and owned by the archbishop of Canterbury. The two villages came together when the archbishop sold East Cheam manor to Henry VIII (one wonders whether he was persuaded to do so) while West Cheam was acquired by the king when he dissolved the cathedral priory.

Cheam continued more or less united for four and a half centuries until a new area began to be developed around the ancient crossroads about a mile north of the old village. With its water supply assured, North Cheam changed from common and agricultural land and began the development which turned it into the bustling centre of today. Cheam Village, as it would have to get used to being called, began to be usurped by its more thrusting neighbour.

Built on neighbouring hills, North Cheam and Cheam Village seem unlikely fellows and are very different in character. Cheam Village is much older, and has had more than its fair share of gentlemen's residences. Apart from Nonsuch Palace and Mansion, there was West Cheam Manor House, where the branch library now stands, and East Cheam Manor later replaced by Lower Cheam House. The latter was built by Mr Antrobus and was situated roughly where Antrobus Close is now. Cheam House stood between The Broadway and Park Lane, Cheam Park House unsurprisingly in Cheam Park and The White House in the High Street where Farnham Court now stands. With the towering bulk of Cheam School at one end of the village and the imposing church on the hill at the other, the village was a compact unit. It had not yet been taken over by urban sprawl, and high-rise buildings, with the exception of churches, were largely unknown. Locals remember looking out of upper windows or from various high spots, and seeing Crystal Palace burning. Watching London burn could not have been strange to a village which would see both the Great Fire and the Blitz.

North Cheam, on the other hand, is a relative newcomer. Developers were not hampered by many old structures or traditional distinctions and, without even many roads to constrict them, had a relatively clean canvas to work with. North Cheam became something of a new town, probably before the phrase was invented, and offered attractive housing at affordable prices. Warner and Watson Ltd., not only built houses with garages but advertised its homes as including: 'the latest swift, automatic boiling and washing machine (in blue enamel).' It's probably no coincidence that Gleeson, one of the largest building contractors in the country, has its headquarters in North Cheam.

The distinction between the two sides of the Cheam coin was blurred during the first quarter of the twentieth century, as North Cheam was just getting off the ground while Cheam Village was virtually demolished and rebuilt. Both are set around crossroads, although that at North Cheam is considerably larger (some would argue not necessarily busier!) Even so, the architectural and cultural styles are quite distinct. South Cheam, while not exactly a backwater, has a tendency to be nostalgic about its more significant past, while North Cheam is less sentimental, more modern and more commercial.

And what of the small valley between the two centres? Again the geology of the area shapes what people do with it. The chalk to the south of Cheam is dotted with small quarries from which locals have hacked out building stone, while the London clay to the north was the site of at least two brick and tile fields. History and geography meet again: Roman tile kilns were found only a few miles to the west in Epsom and Ashtead.

Malden Road, later to become The Broadway, 1891. In the centre, behind the horse and cart, are Acha Cottages, which housed Cheam's first post office. The building on the far left was the latest in a long line of breweries which had been on the site since the twelfth century. It had a deep well, now filled, which yielded very good water and was probably the reason for much of the brewery's success. Further up the road, on the left, can be seen the Old Cottage, which was used as an office for the brewery in the early nineteenth century. Brewing ceased here in about 1910 and the buildings were used for various purposes before being demolished in 1921. The name painted on the horse-drawn cart in the centre of the photograph appears to be 'WSWINES'. A possible connection with the brewery? Judging by the load, probably not! *(Author's collection)*

The Broadway, 20 March 2003. Yes, this really is the same view as in the previous photograph. Little survives of the old buildings, although the cellars of the brewery are still supposed to remain below the piece of grass in front of Travel World's window. The Old Cottage still exists, of course, but has been moved from its original place: the tree further down the road on the left stands next to it. Acha Cottages were on the site of the Abbey National Bank on the far right of the picture. Redevelopment in Cheam village began in 1921 and many of the buildings visible today were completed by 1927. In 1934 the roads were widened and the remodelling of the village was virtually complete. The Broadway is now the centre for shopping in Cheam, but it was not always so. Until the redevelopment most of Cheam's few shops were in the High Street, off to the right in this picture. *(George Hobbs)*

Whitehall, *c.* 1925. No illustrated book of Cheam would be complete without a view of the most important historical building in the village. The old house was built in about 1500 on the site of an earlier structure whose well still survives in the timber-framed building's garden. Three major additions to the original structure give us the building which exists today: the porch, stairs and attic floor were added in about 1550; a three-storey extension including cellar was added to the north-west corner in about 1650; and finally, in 1800, a two-storey extension for kitchen and bathroom plus a lean-to washhouse was added on the south side. *(Author's collection)*

Whitehall, 9 March 2003. Little has changed at Whitehall, for which Cheam has Sutton Borough Council to thank. Members of the Killick family lived in the old house from the mid-eighteenth century until the last of the family died in 1959. In 1963 Whitehall was put on the market and threatened with demolition before the council stepped in and purchased it. The precaution of chalk foundation blocks seems to have been omitted when it came to building the porch, which has consequently sunk several inches. Children visiting Whitehall particularly like the porch room because the dramatic slant so visible from outside is even more noticeable inside. The steep slope of the floor takes unwary visitors by surprise and the few steps to the window become a trot; the return journey a climb. *(George Hobbs)*

The Old Cottage, *c.* 1910. The cottage dates from around 1500 and was built of a pinned oak frame with panels filled with 'rye dough' (clay mixed with rye straw). Many of the timbers are even older, having been adapted for use when the cottage was first constructed. It has been suggested that the building may have been removed from Cuddington village, or built from the timbers of derelict properties when Henry VIII cleared the village to build Nonsuch Palace (see page 29). The photograph is interesting because it displays an early form of re-touching. The lower part of the roof on the left shows a block crudely redrawn. It was altered to disguise a large sign which said 'CYCLE REPAIRS' and, below that, 'TEAS'. *(Author's collection)*

The Old Cottage, 9 March 2003. The building was moved to its present location in 1922 because it impeded the widening of the Broadway. Before it was dismantled it had barge-boarding on the lower storey, but drawings dated from about 1830 do not show barge-boarding so the covering was omitted when it was re-erected. A less forgivable change was the substitution of concrete for the original rye dough in the filling between the timbers of the frame. *(George Hobbs)*

The Broadway, 9 March 2003. The story of Epsom Rural Council buying the Old Cottage and moving it to its present site is well known. What many fail to appreciate, however, is just how far it was moved. The building originally stood just about where the white car is parked in the foreground on the left and a little further into the road. The cottage now stands just behind the tree to the right of the photograph, a distance of about 75 yards from its original site. *(George Hobbs)*

Interior of the Old Cottage, 12 April 2003. The old building is now the home of Cloud 9, which supplies bridal wear; the magnificent gowns and accessories complement the preserved interior wonderfully. The steps on the left lead to a galleried upper floor above which the roof timbers can still be seen. The counter fits neatly underneath the stairs and behind it, left to right, are Maureen Stockley, Tina O'Reilly (proprietor of Cloud 9) and Jennifer Hodges. What a picturesque place to work! *(George Hobbs)*

Malden Road, Good Friday 1919. The occasion is a united open-air service on at the highest point on Malden Road. Between the two houses in the background can just be seen one of the three chimneys for the kilns attached to Cheam brickfields. Bounded on the north and east by Chatsworth Road and Church Hill Road, the brickworks once extended as far as Spring Close Lane and Malden Road. Appropriately enough, the house on the left in this picture was the home of Mr Feast, a local builder. *(Lilian Curd)*

Junction of Lumley Road and Malden Road, 14 June 2003. Rather surprisingly, both of the buildings in the previous photograph still exist. The area where the service was held is now the Esso petrol station and the concrete forecourt covers the area where the priests are celebrating. A large leylandii hedge at the side of the petrol station obscures Lumley Road from the original vantage point, which is why the angle of this view is more acute. Nevertheless, it's still easy to see that the empty spaces have been filled with houses and that the area is far less rural. *(George Hobbs)*

Malden Road, Good Friday 1919. The same open air service, this time looking east towards the spire of St Dunstan's Church. The house behind him was the boyhood home of Mr 'Lol' Sergeant, whose father was the Winston Sergeant who opened the engineering store and cycle shop in the Broadway in 1921 and which only closed in 2003. Lol was a keen scout and later became group scout leader. A group of scouts stand at the front on the right, their hats hanging from their belts. Could Lol be among them? *(Lilian Curd)*

Malden Road, 14 June 2003. The Esso petrol station and Tesco Express store might be new, but the church spire and house both still stand. St Dunstan's graveyard bordered the grounds of West Cheam Manor House, which Elizabeth I granted to John, Lord Lumley, after whom Lumley Road is named. The Queen excepted from the gift the lead and bells of the church: perhaps she thought Lord Lumley might melt them down! *(George Hobbs)*

Love Lane, pre-July 1914. The field on the right is Bourne Hole, called 'Bony Hole' by the locals. 'Bourne' comes from the Old English *burna* meaning spring or stream, and sure enough, in wet weather, the field would flood with spring water. During late 1914 and early 1915 the Sutton District Water Company sought powers from parliament to sink a well and drive adits into Bony Hole. Ewell Parish Council objected to the proposal on the grounds that Bony Hole came within the watershed of the Hog's Mill (now spelt Hogsmill) river and any bourne water extracted would interfere with the water level in the river and impinge on the rights of the riparian owners. Councillor Henderson's impassioned speech was quoted in the *Herald* of 16 January 1915 and stated that he 'thought the company might leave their little stream alone. It was a stream of extreme interest and probably one of the most useful in the kingdom.' *(Lilian Curd)*

Love Lane, 14 June 2003. Houses and trees have changed the lane almost beyond recognition. It's been many years since Bourne water has been seen at Bony Hole, not least because the water company did eventually get permission to drill there. Behind the trees to the right of this picture is a well head from which water is pumped through pipes to a small service reservoir near Cuddington Golf Course. Housing has replaced the trees to the left. The Hogsmill River does still exist, however, running from Bourne Hall in Ewell north-west through Malden to empty into the Thames just south of Kingston Bridge. Councillor Henderson at least would be pleased. *(George Hobbs)*

St Dunstan's Hill, looking south, *c.* 1925. Mrs Mary Mitchell and her elder brother are taking an evening stroll along the footpath which would shortly become the Sutton by-pass. The new road was built in 1929 and relieved the pressure on traffic going through the town. While it was being built a steam shovel – state-of-the-art equipment at the time – worked all night and kept the locals awake. Compared with today there was probably little traffic, but the new road coincided with the development of Cheam generally. In the ten years prior to 1931 the population of Cheam more than doubled, rising from 7,843 in 1921 to 18,510 in 1931. Today Sutton Council lists the population of Cheam as 10,900 but is drawing from a rather smaller geographical area. *(Lilian Curd)*

St Dunstan's Hill, better known as the Sutton bypass, looking south towards Belmont Rise, 14 June 2003. It's impossible now to know exactly where the previous view was taken, but it was somewhere within 50 yards of this spot. The traffic lights mark the intersection of the main access road running north-south, with that running east-west. The original road to Cheam from Sutton crossed about where the photographer is standing and pre-dates even the 1755 Cheam Road (see page 2). It ran from Sutton High Street along Camden Road, Western Road, Tate Road and Love Lane to emerge near St Dunstan's Church. *(George Hobbs)*

Quarry Lodge, with Spot the dog, *c.* 1919. This is the other side of the entrance labelled 'Carriage Drive' in the photograph on page 2. Pictures of Quarry Lodge and the house called The Quarry (see next page) are extremely rare. For a short time this was the home of the Mitchell family who moved to Cheam on 8 February 1919 from a smallholding near Outwood Mill. Mr Mitchell became a gardener at The Quarry but did not enjoy good health. His elder daughter, Winifred, preceded the family to Cheam by becoming under parlour maid at Nonsuch Mansion (see page 31) in 1917. *(Lilian Curd)*

Quarry Park Road leading to Cheam Road, 14 June 2003. The old driveway now forms the part of the road up to the sharp right-hand bend, behind the photographer, where The Quarry was situated. No trace of the lodge appears to remain. Opposite the modern house, and off the photograph to the left, is Quarry Park. It was originally a chalk pit which became known as The Dell after it was abandoned, and was a haven for wild flowers. It was largely filled in and is now a strangely desolate piece of open ground below the surface of Cheam Road. *(George Hobbs)*

The Quarry, *c.* 1919, the home of Mr and Mrs John Seear. Mr Seear was a gold-mining engineer whose wife had once been his housekeeper. In the class-conscious days of Victoria and Edward their alliance was probably the reason why the large house and its occupants were seldom mentioned in contemporary books about Cheam. Mr Seear died in 1929 and left the house and garden to his wife for her lifetime and, on her death, to the parish. The garden is now Seear's Park and still boasts a fine collection of specimen trees. *(Lilian Curd)*

Love Lane with the original rear entrance to The Quarry on the right, 14 June 2003. The wooden gatepost with the chamfered top in the centre of the picture still remains of the two original gateposts to The Quarry's back entrance. Seears Park, formed from The Quarry's garden, is on the left and it is likely that the brick wall is part of the original wall dividing the house from its garden. It sounds an unusual arrangement but Love Lane is one of the oldest trackways in Cheam and there was a public right of way along it. The wall was the early twentieth-century equivalent of net curtains. *(George Hobbs)*

Interior of S.M. Pinegar butcher's shop in Ewell Road, 1970s. Mr Cathie senior is cutting a piece of steak for a customer, while his son Philip is busy in the background. At the time there were only three independently owned freehold shops in Cheam: S.M. Pinegar, W. Sergeant, selling and servicing bicycles and latterly lawnmowers, and Percy Harris the draper. Now only Pinegar's remains.
(*Ron Taylor, Cheam Camera Club*)

Pinegar butcher's shop, 12 April 2003. Now run by Mr Philip Cathie, the butcher's shop has changed very little in the last twenty-five years. It offers old-fashioned service, takes the trouble to fulfil customers' orders and delivers locally using its own van. The shop is rightly popular with its local clientele and takes pride in providing the sort of meat supermarkets won't let you buy. (*George Hobbs*)

Interior of Percy Harris, draper's shop in Station Way, 1970s. Cheam Court Farm used to stand on this site and is remembered in the name of the flats above W.H. Smith and Boots the chemist on the corner of Station Way and Ewell Road. Mr Percy Harris came to Cheam in 1927 and opened his draper's shop in premises next to the Harrow, just about where the traffic lights are now. When the shops were built in Station Way in 1930, Mr Harris moved his draper's business round the corner where the shop remained until it closed. His son, Mr Neville Harris and Mrs Joan North can be seen behind the counter. (*Ron Taylor, Cheam Camera Club*)

Interior of Felicity Hat Hire, Station Way, 24 May 2003. Only the decorated skylight window gives away the fact that these are the same premises. Now, instead of the materials to make fancy articles, the shop stocks the finished item; note the clock on the back wall on the right. Kati Weedon is the proprietor, and two of her colleagues, Hazel King (seated) and Anne Coleman, can be seen discussing the latest batch of finery. (*George Hobbs*)

No. 26 High Street, May 1985. The DIY centre was one of the many premises considered by Oxfam when it was planning to open a charity shop in Cheam. The first such shop in the village, it opened in 1986 and continued, albeit indirectly, Cheam's long tradition of parish charities. Most venerable of these is Smith's Charity dating from 1628 and amounting, at that time, to £4 10s per year. *(Courtesy of Oxfam)*

No. 26 High Street, 23 March 2003. Rising rents caused the Oxfam shop to close on 8 March 2003. A workman removes the newer yellow-on-blue logo to reveal the old-style black-on-white text. Volunteers who manned the shop reacted to the news with mixed feelings, but there was general disappointment that the charity had not communicated its intentions to them directly. The news, like the shop's goods, arrived second-hand. At the time of writing the shop is empty awaiting new occupation. *(George Hobbs)*

United Dairies' Cheam Distributing Depot, Ewell Road, just after it opened, January 1930. *Our Notebook*, the house magazine of United Dairies, reported that a Cheam local paper said 'it is pleasant to see that this company has had in mind the beauty of the rural surroundings of Cheam. Rare in a commercial enterprise, the building not only had extremely up-to-date facilities, which included a canteen, refrigeration plant and drying room for the coats of rain-soaked delivery men but also combined utility with attractiveness. The same local paper went on to say 'the stabling is on the same high standard of efficiency showing that the care and welfare of the horses is being given every attention'. The depot was so proud of its facilities that United Dairies offered to show round anyone interested in modern milk distribution. *(Courtesy of Dairy Crest)*

Cheam Distributing Depot, Ewell Road, 9 March 2003. United Dairies and Cow & Gate merged in 1959 to become Unigate Dairies, which itself was taken over by Dairy Crest in 2000. The depot closed on 1 February 2003 and the management of milk rounds moved to Epsom, Surbiton and Wimbledon depots. Apart from new gates, a tree and the tarmacing of the increasingly busy road, very little has outwardly changed. *(George Hobbs)*

Forge Lane, *c.* 1980s. The light-coloured building in the distance is the Railway Inn between which and the new houses in the foreground is an old quarry. The village smithy, the forge of which still exists as a private house next to the railway bridge in Station Way, was first situated in this quarry. Its owner, Moses Barnes, was one in a long line of family blacksmiths and built the Station Way premises in 1860. He presumably moved his business because it was more convenient for passing trade, but the old forge is still commemorated in the name of the road. *(Ron Taylor, Cheam Camera Club)*

Forge Lane, 12 April 2003. The chimney pots of the Railway Inn can still just be seen to the left of the photograph. The pub has an unusual choice of inn sign as it depicts an electric train rather than the ubiquitous steam locomotive of most inn signs. Perhaps the landlord is continuing a tradition, as the sign's previous incarnation showed all the details of a country station, including milk churns, bench and cat – but no train. *(George Hobbs)*

Warren Cottage, pre-1930. A very rare photograph of a cottage, demolished in 1930, which stood at the entrance to an 11-acre enclosure surrounded by an 8 ft high brick wall. Holes appear at intervals around the wall through which beaters would drive hares to the riders and dogs waiting on the other side. It's an interesting idea, and may well be true, but the holes seem rather small for the average hare to squeeze through. Some parts of the wall are Tudor and connections have been suggested with Nonsuch Park and Palace, about 2 miles away. (*Author's collection*)

The corner of Warren Avenue and Onslow Avenue, 9 March 2003. Judging from old documents, which show a lodge at the north-east corner, Warren Cottage probably stood on this the north-west corner. It is tempting to think that the gateway on view is the building's original doorway. Despite the wishes of various developers, Warren Copse, the small woodland at the centre of the enclosure, still exists divided between the houses whose back gardens now make up the hare warren. The Hare Wall itself is now a listed building. (*George Hobbs*)

Nonsuch Palace excavations, September 1959. The base of the south-east tower. The foundations of the palace were a mixture of chalk blocks and dressed stone. Only the lower part of the foundation of the tower remained as stones from the outside east wall of the palace had been removed for other building. *(Derek Poulter)*

Nonsuch Park, 20 March 2003. After the excavations the site was backfilled to preserve the remains. The foundations were mostly of chalk, which is the local bedrock and, as chalk does not withstand frost and damp well, the remains would have needed expensive preservative treatment every few years. If covered, the remains are preserved for future generations should they develop new archaeological techniques and wish to have another look at them. The only visible indications on the surface are three pillars positioned at the north and south ends of the palace and in the middle. The figure in the foreground is standing just above where the base of the south-east tower is buried. *(George Hobbs)*

Nonsuch Palace excavations, September 1959. The steps mark the entrance to the wine-cellar, which measured 18 ft x 68 ft, and was the largest single room excavated. The walls were made of stone from Merton Priory, which was about 4 miles away; they still stood more than 6 ft high in places. The floor was cobbled and is just visible at the bottom of the steps. The hole to the right of the steps and three-quarters of the way up the wall, originally contained a lead pipe for running water. (Derek Poulter)

Nonsuch Park, 20 March 2003. The pillar on the left is the middle one of the three marking the palace range. The photographer of the modern picture is standing in approximately the same place as the photographer of the 1959 shot. The figure to the right marks the position of the steps. The trees in the near background have grown up since the excavation, but the range on the skyline corresponds in both photographs. Tales still abound of an underground link between Whitehall (see page 11) and Nonsuch Palace, but no trace has ever been found. The excavation did discover, however, a series of very large sewers, which could have been mistaken for a network of small tunnels. (George Hobbs)

Nonsuch Palace excavations, September 1959. Probably the kitchen foundations from the north. The kitchen wing was about 135 ft long with a courtyard in front of it. The first wall, which runs the width of the photograph, is probably the north wall of the kitchen buildings. The excavation of the kitchen unearthed a large number of animal and poultry bones, oyster shells, charcoal and small metal objects. *(Derek Poulter)*

Nonsuch Park, 20 March 2003. The author standing in the middle of a large field! Nonsuch Park is managed jointly by the London Borough of Sutton, into which Cheam falls, and Epsom & Ewell Borough Council. It is a large, pleasant open area which attracts walkers, joggers and locals who want to escape from the ever-increasing roar of traffic. One of the keepers' cottages is visible in the background. The modern picture is taken, as closely as possible, from the same place as the 1959 photograph: the tripod in the foreground marks the probable position of the first wall; the figure the likely position of the second. *(George Hobbs)*

Nonsuch Palace excavations, September 1959. Much of the stone used for building Nonsuch Palace came from Merton Priory, which was used as a local source of stone. Demolition started even before the priory was officially surrendered and, in all, 3,600 tons of priory stone was reused in Henry VIII's palace. This 10 inch lion gargoyle came from Merton Priory and, as with other carved blocks, was used as hardcore. The lion spent more than four centuries upside down in the palace foundations but seems to have suffered remarkably little damage. *(Derek Poulter)*

Nonsuch Park, 20 March 2003. Only the stone markers indicate where the palace is and even they are deceptive, appearing to be much smaller than they are – look at the figure by the middle one. A plan of the palace appears on the pillar at the south end and is just visible in the photograph. The largest of the trees between the two nearest pillars marks the approximate position of the sanctuary of Cuddington parish church. In 1538 church and village were swept away by Henry VIII who wanted the land to build Nonsuch Palace. The parish itself, however, survived for another 450 years, only being divided between Ewell and Cheam in 1933. In so rural an area the Church of England presumably felt that the lack of a parish church didn't matter too much. Even so, one or two residents of the Cheam part of the old Cuddington parish still talk about the trouble they had during the war persuading the local vicar to marry them as 'we weren't in his parish, you know!' *(George Hobbs)*

Nonsuch Palace excavations, September 1959. The excavation ran from 6 July to 28 September 1959 during which over 60,000 people visited the site. Volunteer guides conducted parties around the excavation and this transportable polling station was pressed into service as a small museum. The temporary shelter opened its doors on Saturday 18 July 1959, charging 6d admission. More than 26,000 people viewed the historical display and selection of recent finds. *(Derek Poulter)*

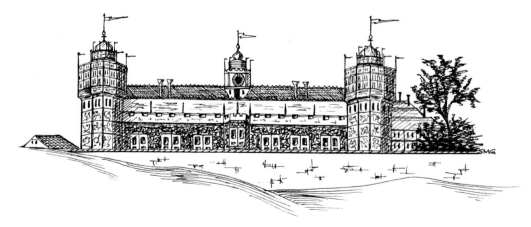

Nonsuch Palace, after a print by Joris Hoefnagel, 1582. The original is in the British Museum; this is one of the many copies. The view looks north that is the opposite way from the modern picture on the previous page, and the palace appears over the top of the garden wall. Formal gardens were something of a status symbol and Nonsuch Palace saw the introduction of the first lilac and water lily to be grown in this country. The excavations of the base of the right-hand tower in this picture are shown on page 26. The kitchen range (see page 28) is just visible as the rather less imposing buildings on the right. It was from pictures such as this that archaeologists made their first estimations about what they would find on the site. *(Author's collection)*

Nonsuch Mansion, 20 March 2003. The Mansion House was built during 1731–43 by Joseph Thompson, but sold in 1799 to Samuel Farmer, who employed Jeffrey Wyatt to rebuild it in Tudor Gothic. Amateur photographers will recognise the building as the one which the magazine *Amateur Photographer*, for a time based in Ewell Road, used to photograph to test camera lenses newly released on to the market. (*George Hobbs*)

St Mary's Church, Cuddington, Worcester Park, 21 April 2003. Nonsuch Palace was surrounded by two parks. The Little Park of 671 acres included the palace itself, most of what is now Cheam Village and the warren (see page 25). The Great Park consisted of 911 acres, the keeper of which was the Earl of Worcester who eventually gave the area its modern name of Worcester Park. In August 1894 the foundation stone of St Mary's was laid to create an historic link with the church demolished in what was to become Nonsuch Park (see page 29). Under the stone is an inscription, part of which reads: 'a new church, built to replace a former church which was destroyed in the early parts of the 16th century . . .'. (*George Hobbs*)

Diana's Dyke, Nonsuch Park, 4 March 1930. Strictly speaking Diana's Dyke was the name given to part of the Grove of Diana, which was south and west of Nonsuch Palace and now very difficult to find as it is covered with trees. This photograph is of part of the Long Ditch north of the palace site and close to where it is thought the palace stables were: the old name is occasionally used erroneously. In wet seasons, bourne or spring water rose in the Long Ditch, eventually draining away through a culvert to the Hogsmill river. The 1930s were particularly wet and water lay in this area for many months. At the time the Sutton District Water Company were seeking new supplies of fresh water for the rapidly increasing housing stock in the area. It is possible that the water company considered the bourne water visible in the Long Ditch as a potential supply. *(Courtesy of Sutton and East Surrey Water)*

Long Ditch, Nonsuch Park, 15 June 2003. The ditch is one of the very few areas of Nonsuch Park which is not flat, and so is not mown. The water table has been lowered considerably over the last couple of decades, and bourne water in the Long Ditch is now very rare but the additional traces of moisture may be encouraging the trees to flourish. Tradition says that the ditch was originally dug as part of a moat around Nonsuch Palace, but this is now generally thought to be unlikely. Not only would it have been rather a long way from the palace buildings, but is downhill from the site: the rest of the moat, had it existed, would have had to be extremely deep indeed. It's possible that the ditch had something to do with the stable block, or was perhaps an ambitious drainage channel. Whatever it is, it's too regular to be anything other than man made. *(George Hobbs)*

North Cheam crossroads, looking north-east, 24 May 2003. Compare this view with that on pages 34–5. One hundred years ago most of this area was fields. *The History of St Mary's Church, Cuddington* says: 'in 1903, an eight-year-old boy called Albert Puttock saw a church on a hill across the fields from his small cottage near North Cheam crossroads'. The church was St Mary's in Worcester Park on top of the next hill along. It has no tower and only a very small spire (see page 31). There must have been very few buildings in the way for young Albert to be able to see it. *(George Hobbs)*

Queen Victoria pub, 29 March 2003. The area around the North Cheam crossroads was mostly common land. Two main arterial roads, running roughly east-west and north-south crossed near this point. Until about 1882 a turnpike or toll gate used to stand on the Malden Road very near the North Cheam crossroads, and not far from the pub in the photograph. When the first battle between the Royalist and Parliamentary armies took place in Worcester Park in 1643, Royalist troops, defeated and confused, fled across the common, over the crossroads and down through the village. According to parish records three of them only made it so far and are buried in St Dunstan's churchyard. *(George Hobbs)*

North Cheam crossroads, 1924. Local resident, Mr Steptoe, came to live in Cheam Common Road as a boy in 1924 and says 'talking about old times made me cast my memory back and do these drawings. Development was soon to be on the move. . . . Sutton by-pass was built about 1926, then the various farms in the area were sold for new roads and houses. Before that, there were no shops within half a mile of the cross roads, but the small garage which was in one of the fields was moved nearer the crossroads and shops started to be built.' Lavender's Farm, at the top of the picture, is now a housing estate, but is remembered in the street names, Lavender Avenue and Farm Way. (B. Steptoe)

North Cheam crossroads, 1994. The A2043 approaches from the south and crosses the A24 London Road. South of the crossroads the A2043 is Malden Road; it becomes Cheam Common Road north of the junction. Mr Steptoe continues, 'the old Queen Victoria pub was demolished in 1936 and a new larger one built which in turn was demolished in 1964. An even newer, smaller version was incorporated into the commercial development [in the bottom right corner]' (see page 33). *(B. Steptoe)*

London Transport Executive Sports Ground, London Road, September 1934. Few people realise that London Transport purchased a sports ground in North Cheam for the use of its staff. Land was relatively cheap in the suburbs and getting to the sports ground was easy for staff with concessionary travel permits. This view looks south west, with London Road running up the slight rise towards the large tree. To the right is a row of shops, with their awnings extended. *(London's Transport Museum)*

Sports Ground, London Road, 24 May 2003. The tennis courts still exist and are situated just behind the photographer, but access to that part of the ground is now restricted. The row of shops is also still there, but now faces a much larger rival; the south-west corner of the ground is now the site of Sainsbury's supermarket. The store is just visible behind the trees which form the north-eastern boundary to its car park. *(George Hobbs)*

London Transport Executive Sports Ground, London Road, September 1934. This view, looking north east, emphasises the huge ground the various sports had at their disposal. New housing is visible to the right and the area is gradually assuming the bustle it has today. Note the AEC NS-type bus. Everyone had their own opinion about why the new buses were given a two-character designation, while all the earlier ones had only one. The explanation which seems most appropriate for Cheam was that NS stood for 'None Superior' – a second Nonsuch in fact. *(London's Transport Museum)*

Sports Ground, London Road, 24 May 2003. New dwellings still seem to be the order of the day as a row of houses has been built within what was the sports ground perimeter. Although building around the edges of the sports ground has reduced the area by about half it's still a very useful open space in what is now densely populated commuter belt. Local teams still organise fixtures to be played on the ground on a regular basis and the tall light to the left illuminates an all-weather pitch. *(George Hobbs)*

Foundations for new Sainsbury store, 562 London Road, 1971. The store is being built on the south-west corner of what was part of the London Transport Executive Sports Ground (see page 36). The contractors were Bernard Sunley and Sons plc, now part of the Sunley Turriff Group. There's not much to see as yet, but it's quite an impressive hole in the ground. *(G. Hana Photography Ltd)*

Sainsbury's, 562 London Road, 5 April 2003. The photographer received some very strange looks as he took this excellent view of Sainsbury's dustbins! This is the second Sainsbury's to be built on the site and dates from 1993. The chimneys and roofs of the backs of the houses in Senhouse Road, visible in the upper picture, can just be seen over the top of Sainsbury's side wall. *(George Hobbs)*

Entrance to Sainsbury's, 562 London Road, 1971. Taken shortly after the store opened on 13 July, this photograph shows that the supermarket is already well patronised. Shopping customs changed so much, even in twenty years, that by 1993 the 'new' store had become too small. It was demolished and replaced by another Sainsbury's on the same site. (*The Sainsbury Archive*)

Entrance to Sainsbury's, 562 London Road, 5 April 2003. Opened in September 1993, the current branch is much bigger than that which preceded it. Not only does the store now stock a huge variety and quantity of items but the lighting is much more sympathetic. In this Sainsbury's are upholding the dying wish of John James Sainsbury, the founder of the firm. His last words are said to have been: 'keep the shops well lit'. (*George Hobbs*)

No. 485 London Road, 21 April 2003. John James Sainsbury died in 1928 and so did not see the shop which bears his name open here in North Cheam in November 1936. Within three years the new outlet was plunged into the intricacies of rationing. The Ministry of Food was responsible for ensuring fair distribution of foodstuffs at reasonable prices and Sainsbury's set up a system of 'contact clerks' who telephoned selected branches as soon as they had been notified by the Ministry of a change in the regulations. So efficient was the contact clerk system that local food officers found it quicker to telephone the Sainsbury rationing office than go through their own complicated official channels. The North Cheam branch of Sainsbury's remained in this building until 1971, when it moved to new premises further along London Road (see page 38). (*George Hobbs*)

Sainsbury's tessellated floor, The Broadway, Cheam, 21 April 2003. The Sainsbury's in Cheam Village was built between 1930 and 1934 on a site carefully chosen as being in the centre of a parade. John James Sainsbury thought corner sites more difficult to keep cool and clean and dismissed them as 'for banks'. He was one of the early traders to devise a housestyle and mosaic floors complemented by glazed ceramic tiles were routinely installed in all shops. The North Cheam branch, in the building pictured above, would almost certainly once have had such a pavement. The tiles and tesserae were produced and laid by Minton Hollins employing Italian craftsmen. The former Sainsbury's in Cheam Village is now a furniture shop, but the splendid floor and wall tiling still remains. (*George Hobbs*)

2

Serving the People

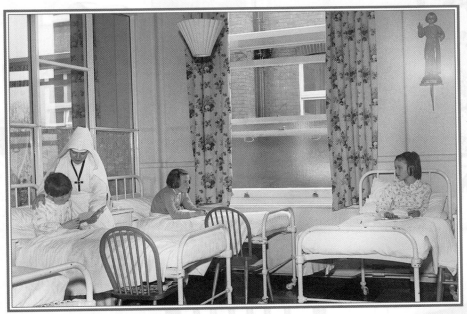

St Anthony's Hospital, *c.* 1960. A new children's ward was opened in August 1956 and considered to be state-of-the-art for the time. At the end of 1956 the ward was indirectly responsible for a temporary closure which threatened the hospital, when one of the children admitted was diagnosed as having poliomyelitis. The entire children's ward, including fourteen nurses and Sister Mary Edmund, was placed under quarantine on 2 January 1957. No one was allowed to leave the ward and eating and sleeping arrangements were challenging to say the least. All patients and staff were pronounced clear of the disease by 18 January and the hospital managed to stay open. Children continued to be treated at St Anthony's for many years but now the hospital concentrates on adult care. (© *Nursing Times and courtesy of St Anthony's Hospital*)

Once somewhere to live and the basics of food, warmth and shelter are sorted out, people look to their spiritual and physical wellbeing. Religion looks after the spirit, education the mind and healthcare the body. Cheam has a good selection of churches, schools and hospitals, many combining the different functions within one establishment. The area has a hospital and hospice founded and run by Roman Catholic nuns, a couple of nursing homes founded and run by a Presbyterian church and a school founded and run by a Church of England curate, many of whose successors were also clergymen.

St Anthony's Hospital and St Raphael's Hospice at the north end of Cheam share a similar philosophy with St Andrew's nursing homes at the south: looking after people's welfare cannot be compartmentalised. St Mary's Church of England Children's Home, which existed in Sandy Lane until it closed in about 1960, had a similar attitude. On a grander scale, so did Cheam School. A boarding school must ensure that its pupils remain happy and healthy as well as training their minds. Before Cheam School had its own chapel the boys went to services at the parish church. At that time seats in church had to be paid for and the school charged parents 10s when their son entered the school to guarantee the boy space on a pew. The school had one of the galleries of the old St Dunstan's Church (see page 44) reserved for pupils' use. Boys as young as seven would board and, inevitably, some would be homesick. Former domestic staff at the school remember that each evening they had to ensure that the right teddy went into the right bed.

St Dunstan's is unusual in the area as it is the only church to be built on top of a hill. Pre-Christian religious settlements were often on hilltops, and when Christianity was introduced the Church pragmatically adopted already well-used religious sites. Such could have been the case in Cheam. The site has certainly been in use since Saxon times, although there have been at least three major alterations with large parts of the church extensively rebuilt. During the last of the major changes, in 1864, a thirteenth-century stone coffin was discovered when the square tower was demolished. It contained the skeleton of a man, presumably a priest, with a pewter chalice and paten beside him. Grave goods are usually associated with earlier pagan burials, but the custom lingered in rural backwaters. Cheam may now be inside the Greater London boundary, but 800 years ago would have been a tiny hamlet tucked against the wilderness which was the North Downs. Perhaps the man was well loved in the village and his congregation wanted to show their respect.

As Cheam Village and North Cheam developed, the area needed new churches, schools and hospitals to serve the growing population. St Dunstan's has two daughter churches, St Alban's and St Oswald's, the latter built fifty years ago to serve a new housing development built on land previously occupied by Brock's firework factory. There are two Roman Catholic churches in the area, St Christopher's in Cheam Village and St Cecilia's in North Cheam. The Baptist community is well represented and other denominations are flourishing.

Cheam School may no longer be in Cheam, but the village was its home and the church its inspiration for almost 250 years. Private schools probably started with a scholarly parson wanting to provide some education for his own sons and unable to afford private tuition. There were far more curates than parishes and preferment relied on patronage, so expanding his efforts to teach the sons of the gentry in his parish would have provided a clergyman with the means of supplementing his stipend. Teaching would have been a good if precarious way of making a living; teachers today might say that little has changed. Certainly in 1645, the first date at which the school can be proved to exist, Cheam School's headmaster was a Doctor of Divinity, George Aldritch. Headmasters continued to be clerics all the time the school was in Cheam, partly because religious tests were still part of the entrance examination to Oxford and Cambridge universities.

Education has changed out of all recognition since Cheam School was founded during the Stuart dynasty. At that time girls were thought to be less in need of an education and were taught by their mothers, sent to an all-girls boarding school or occasionally instructed by female governesses. It's only within the last hundred years or so that education for girls has been taken seriously, and only within the last few decades that education for both sexes has been formalised. Cheam has seen examples of many of the different types of educational establishment. Apart from its most famous school there have been several other private schools in Cheam, including Mr Brown's in Stafford House, Park Road, and Ambleside School in West Drive. There was also a charity school, opened to both boys and girls, in 1826, and built on ground given by Mr Palmer, owner of Cheam Park. The District School, as it was called, fronted on to Malden Road, near what is now Netley Close, and taught basic reading and practical subjects. It later became Malden Road Boys School but was demolished in 1993. A row of houses now occupies the site.

Cheam has something of a tradition of caring for those in need. Mr John Fiddyment rented part of Cheam Park and used it to provide treats, in the form of amusements and picnics, for children from the East End. An entry in the Cheam rate book for 4 October 1741 states that £2 – a lot of money – had been 'paid Stephen Bundell for a fortnight nursing Bridgett Pullen in ye smallpox'. The area continues to be particularly fortunate in the quality of its healthcare. Apart from having one of the best-respected private hospitals in the country, Cheam also has a large number of privately run nursing homes. In one sense, St Anthony's Hospital continues a much earlier method of serving the people. The earliest hospital building took over the premises of the local hostelry.

St Dunstan's Church, pre-1864. The church stood on the south side of the present building, incorporated the Lumley Chapel, which is now a separate building, and extended westwards nearly as far as the lych gate. The porch, although appearing to be stone, was actually made of wood, the tower had a clock face only in its south side and what appears to be a buttress protruding almost in the centre of the photograph is actually an external staircase to the west gallery. In 1862 the decision was taken to replace the church with an entirely new building, the church pictured still being used for worship during construction. Once the new building had been consecrated the whole of the old church, with the exception of the Lumley Chapel, was demolished. *(Author's collection)*

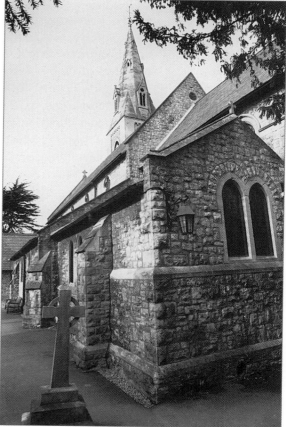

St Dunstan's Church, 9 March 2003. Designed by Frederick Hyde Pownall, the church was built in 1864 in the French Gothic style of six centuries earlier. Cheam once belonged to the cathedral priory of Christchurch, Canterbury, and it is likely that Canterbury founded the church. St Dunstan, the leading saint in Canterbury until he was displaced by Thomas Becket in the twelfth century, lived from 909 to 988 AD and was the archbishop and statesman largely responsible for reviving English monasticism. When Edgar the Peaceful was crowned in 957, it was Dunstan who modified the coronation rite for the ceremony and his modification remains the basis for the modern service. St Dunstan is traditionally regarded as a craftsman, so it is fitting that much of the interior of the church, particularly the tiles behind the altar and the gold-starred Victorian ceiling, is in the Arts and Crafts style. The other local building designed by F.H. Pownall was Banstead Lunatic Asylum, now the site of High Down and Down View prisons. *(George Hobbs)*

St Dunstan's Church bell tower, probably 1977. Although the church was built in 1864, the tower and spire were not completed until 1871. During that year a ring of six bells was installed, which was rung between 1896 and 1918. Even so, church officials were obviously unhappy as, in 1922, bellfounders Gillett and Johnston Ltd, a firm which still exists in Croydon, were called in to assess matters. Their report concurred with official worries by saying baldly that: 'the bells all swing in the same direction and there is a crack in the tower'. The bells were thus condemned to decades of silence. In 1977 repositioning the bell frames and a complete overhaul meant that the bells could sound for the first time in over fifty years. 'They had clear, loud, lusty, sounding voices, had these Bells; and far and wide they might be heard upon the wind' as Dickens wrote in *The Chimes* about another St Dunstan's Church, St Dunstan-in-the-West, Fleet Street which is only 12 or so miles away. This and the following photograph show one of the bells being hoisted into position in the bell tower. *(Ron Taylor, Cheam Camera Club)*

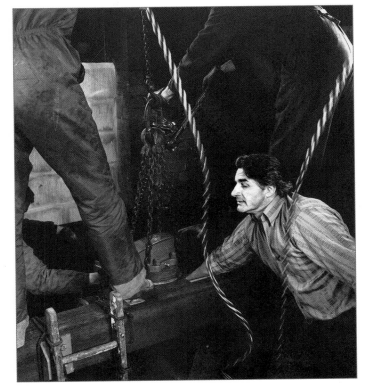

St Dunstan's Church bell tower, probably 1977. Church bells are rung by being swung through slightly more than 360 degrees. The mouth of the bell swings about the stock, which in the photograph is the part around which the chains are wrapped to lift the bell. Bells can weigh anything from a couple of hundred pounds to several tons each and take about two seconds to rotate. Playing a recognisable tune is therefore impossible or at best very difficult. Change ringing, the tumbling sound synonymous with church bells in this country, evolved in England in the early part of the seventeenth century. It involves each bell sounding in a precise order to make a sequential and changing pattern of sound. In *The Nine Tailors* Dorothy L. Sayers says 'the art of change ringing is peculiar to the English and, like most English peculiarities, unintelligible to the rest of the world'. There are however one or two groups in the US and Australia who are in sympathy with English peculiarities. *(Ron Taylor, Cheam Camera Club)*

Lumley Chapel, 8 April 2003. The chapel was the chancel of the pre-1864 church, and was probably part of the church as originally founded: there are signs of early Norman and Saxon work in the blocked windows on the north side. Lord Lumley arranged the chapel as a family mausoleum to contain his own tomb and those of his two wives. When the old church was pulled down all the memorial tablets were moved into the chapel, so that it now offers a fascinating window into the lives and deaths of important Cheam families.

The current head of the Lumley family is Richard Aldred Lumley, 12th Earl of Scarborough. The Lumley Chapel is now in the care of the Churches Conservation Trust and has recently been restored. It remains a consecrated building and the occasional service is still held before its tiny altar. *(George Hobbs)*

Interior of Lumley Chapel, 12 April 2003. This is the tomb of the second Lady Lumley which faces her predecessor across the nave. The position of the tomb can be determined from outside the chapel as it is under the small roof halfway down the wall on the north side. Apart from the grand tombs the chapel has a magnificent plaster roof, several interesting memorials, including plaques to Messrs Peach and Northey, and a palimpsest, which is a memorial the brass of which has been reused from an earlier memorial and is therefore incised on both sides. The original Lord Lumley would be pleased to know that the Lumley Chapel is being preserved as an antiquity since he was one of the earliest members of the Society of Antiquaries founded in the reign of Elizabeth I. *(George Hobbs)*

St Andrew's Church, laying the foundation stone of Miles Hall, 18 June 1927. From 30 January 1925 up to fifty people had met once a month for a service held in the lounge of Mr D.N. Shaw of Gwyder Lodge, York Road. The 'Drawing Room Church' wanted to found a new church building in the area and, after much searching, finally selected a site on the corner of Northey Avenue and The Avenue. Neither road as yet had a name, but not so the church. The committee resolved on St Andrew as a patron saint, based, so it is said, on that fact that, as St Andrew was noted for bringing others to Christ, that should also be the aim of this church. The foundation stone was laid at 3.00 p.m. by Mr L.G. Sloan, convenor of the Presbyterian extension scheme. Appropriately the event included the singing of the hymn 'This stone in faith we lay'. *(Courtesy of St Andrew's Church)*

Miles Hall, 24 May 2003. In 1967, the hall was named to honour St Andrew's first minister, the Revd Edwin Griffith Miles who served the church from 1928 to 1944. Known affectionately as 'Padre', he worked tirelessly with young people and saw the new St Andrew's as primarily a teaching church. He would undoubtedly have been delighted that the Miles Hall is now used for mother and toddler groups, youth groups and as a meeting place for people of all ages. *(George Hobbs)*

Below: St Andrew's Church, cutting the first sod,
25 July 1932. These two photographs should be viewed in
sequence after those on page 50 but the layout of the
book dictates that they must appear here. The outline of
the church is clearly marked by tape on poles and the
photograph was probably taken from the roof of the Miles
Hall. Thinking had moved on since the building of the
hall, particularly with the appointment of 'Padre' Miles.
The original design was thought to be too traditional and,
more controversially still, too small. Mr Miles wanted a
church filled with light and air, writing 'this . . . is a new
Church for the post-war generation of the twentieth
century; therefore it should have no suggestion of gloom'.
(*Courtesy of St Andrew's Church*)

Above: St Andrew's Church, laying the foundation stone, 22 October 1932. Bricks were laid by members of the Congregational Union, Salvation Army, Methodist Union, Presbyterian Church of England, Baptist Association and Church of England in an ecumenical gesture of support for the new congregation. Note the solitary, caped policeman combining crowd control with point duty on the unmade road. The new design for the church was produced by Maxwell Ayrton, who also designed the Wembley Stadium of the British Empire Exhibition, Twickenham Bridge, St Werburgh's Row of shops in Chester and the National Institute of Medical Research. The four-sided arch visible in the picture is a motif found throughout the church and produces a very real sense of unity (see page 51). *(Courtesy of St Andrew's Church)*

Miles Hall, early in 1928. The hall was opened for worship on 18 December 1927 at an inaugural service led by Revd Dr R.C. Gillie, Minister of Marylebone Presbyterian Church. Critics thought the hall too large and ill sited on an unmade, unlit road, but more than 200 people crowded into it for the opening service. Mrs Rankin, a member of the 'Drawing Room Church' (see page 47) wrote in her diary: 'cold, icy wind today. . . . Crowds going in and we were fortunate to get a good seat.' (*Courtesy of St Andrew's Church*)

Miles Hall, 5 April 2003. The hall now forms the central structure in a complex of buildings, which, in plan, is shaped as the letter E (see page 52). In the background to the right is the Aitken Hall and, in the centre of the photograph and behind the Aitken Hall, the roof and windows of the Tweddle Hall. The latter was named after David Tweddle, leader of the original nine people instrumental in getting St Andrew's started. The architects of Miles Hall, Matley, Brotherton and Mills, had also designed a church in the same style, to be built to its east. However, the firm moved to Manchester so another architect, Maxwell Ayrton (see pages 48–9), was appointed. (*George Hobbs*)

St Andrew's Church under construction with Miles Hall in the foreground, autumn 1932. A cruciform shape large enough to seat 600 people was not feasible on the land available, so the church was designed largely as a rectangle, with a four-sided arch-shaped apse at the south end. Frames for lancet windows of a similar shape can just be seen in the skeleton of the church in the photograph. Interestingly, there is no curved line in any part of the building; the whole is designed using only flat lines and surfaces. (*Courtesy of St Andrew's Church*)

St Andrew's Church, 5 April 2003. The church building was opened on 8 July 1933. The building escaped damage during the war, although it had at least one near miss. The church annual report for 1940 mentioned that two large land mines, suspended from parachutes, had caught in some trees on Wilbury Avenue. Both were rendered harmless by a bomb disposal squad. Today St Andrew's is the centre of a thriving community. Its building, modern even by twenty-first century standards, combines the solidity of tradition with a real sense of looking to the future. (*George Hobbs*)

Aitken Hall, construction, 18 April 1963. Begun on 17 February 1963, Aitken Hall was designed by Neville Hinwood and named after Mrs Jessie Aitken, an early church member. Mrs Rankin wrote in her diary (see page 50): 'Tuesday, 6th December 1927. Met Mrs Galloway and Mrs Aitken at Holts and bought china for work party teas. We chose a pretty pattern called the Parrot design [the church still has some of this china]. Mrs Aitken paid for two complete sets and then at Walkers paid for two dozen tea spoons (well done, Mrs Aitken!)' Well done indeed! (*Courtesy of St Andrew's Church*)

St Andrew's Church and halls, 1983. The photograph shows the full range of facilities with which St Andrew's Church serves the local community. To the left is the church itself, with its strikingly modern appearance, rising above all surrounding buildings. In the centre is the Miles Hall, the oldest building on the site and reflecting an earlier period of design. To the right is the completed Aitken Hall which is in constant use by the church and outside societies. The complex is always bustling with life and well justifies 'Padre' Miles's prophetic remark, in 1933: 'if you haven't the faith to build what is necessary, don't build at all.' (*Courtesy of St Andrew's Church*)

St Paul's, Howell Hill, 8 July, probably 1962. St Paul's owes its beginning to the vision and generosity of Archdeacon Newill, whose 'road to Damascus' was the road to Cheam. In 1928 he was travelling between Cheam and Ewell when he saw the beginnings of a housing development and realised that the new residents would need a church. He therefore bought them a field to build it on. Even then the first church was not built on the site until over thirty years later. In 1963 a wooden prefabricated building was erected for the growing congregation, which until then had been squeezing into each other's homes for regular services. The photograph shows cutting the first sod of the temporary church building. *(Courtesy of St Paul's, Howell Hill)*

St Paul's vicarage, 27 April 2003. There have been three churches on Archdeacon Newill's site. The main church building required a much larger area than the temporary accommodation and was built further down the hill, leaving the original site to the vicarage. The vagaries of civil parish boundaries means that St Paul's, Howell Hill, is just over the border and therefore technically in Epsom and Ewell, although geographically it belongs as much to Cheam.
(George Hobbs)

St Paul's, Howell Hill, *c.* 1970. The first permanent church building was a wooden Scandinavian-type structure with a brick-built hall behind it. Behind the church on the right, facing Northey Avenue, is the vicarage. Before the new church was built Terry Reed, a sixteen-year-old living in Cheyham Gardens, constructed a scale model of it, so that the congregation could see what it would look like. With room to seat 280 people, the church was designed by David Nye, architect for the diocese of Southwark, and dedicated by the Bishop of Guildford on 30 November 1963. *(Courtesy of St Paul's, Howell Hill)*

Demolition of St Paul's, Howell Hill, 1988. During the 1970s and '80s St Paul's congregation expanded beyond the capacity of their church building. Services were held simultaneously in the church and main hall and discussions about expansion were replaced by talk of demolition and rebuilding. A larger church was needed so the St Paul's community decided to build one. The last service in the Scandinavian-type building took place on 13 September 1987. *(Courtesy of St Paul's, Howell Hill)*

Lowering the lantern light on to the new building,
St Paul's, Howell Hill, 21 February 1989. The lantern
light is situated over the altar and tops off a huge
stainless steel roof. The new building was strikingly
modern in appearance, designed by Boyce Kemp and
Bron of Eastbourne and built by R. Durtnell & Sons Ltd,
the oldest building company in the country. Founded in
1591, Durtnell has been run by the same family for
twelve generations. Appropriately, the first complete
building erected by founders of the firm, brothers John
and Brian, was a rectory called Poundsbridge Manor in
Kent. It was completed in 1593 and still stands.
(Courtesy of St Paul's, Howell Hill)

Below: St Paul's, Howell Hill, 27 April 2003. Compare
this view with the one at the top of the previous page
and the difference in size is immediately apparent.
The building faces the roundabout on the junction of
Cheam Road with Northey Avenue and is particularly
impressive when approached from the west. The
church was used for the first time on Easter morning,
26 March 1989, and formally consecrated by the
bishop of Guildford on 15 April the same year.
(George Hobbs)

Interior of St Paul's, Howell Hill, *c. 1970.* The Scandinavian-type building is tent-like and based on the use of Utile portal frames and low brick walls in a traditional cruciform. The architect, David Nye, was mindful of the need to provide an effective place for worship at a reasonable price and produced many similar church designs; the interior of the church of Christ the King at Redhill is very similar to St Paul's, Howell Hill, as it was. Although only existing for twenty-four years, the building saw the congregation more than treble in size from just under 100 to well over 300 by the time it closed. *(Courtesy of St Paul's, Howell Hill)*

Interior of St Paul's, Howell Hill, 1989. The current church interior has changed very little since it was completed. It gives the impression of great space and simplicity and, with movable seating and a movable dais, was designed to provide maximum flexibility and visibility. The 9 ft diameter circular wall hanging behind the altar is a striking focal point and was designed and made by Jean Hammond of Tollers Design. Jean comments: 'the position of the hanging meant that, during services, figures would move across the image and be directly in front of it. I therefore deliberately chose a non-figurative image and a symmetrical design. I saw the design working as a backcloth to the ministry going on in front of it. . . .' *(Courtesy of R. Durtnell & Sons Ltd)*

St Alban's choir, corner of Elmbrook Road and Gander Green Lane, c. 1924. The rector and church-wardens of St Dunstan's Church, Cheam, identified the need for a church to minister to the east of the parish and founded a mission church on a corner site in Elmbrook Road. The first building on the site was of corrugated iron and some of St Dunstan's congregation went along to help out. This is the first choir at St Alban's. The names of the boys are no longer known, but in the back row, left to right, are Mr Rapier, lay reader, and Miss Boxall, Sunday School superintendent. *(Lilian Curd)*

St Alban's, Gander Green Lane, 15 June 2003. Looking much older than its eighty-odd years, St Alban's was constructed from the timbers of Cheam Court farmhouse after it was demolished in 1929. Architect and local historian Charles Marshall commented that the rector and churchwardens were 'thus able to construct a church, at a low cost, that already had a tradition attached to it, and much of the atmosphere and colouring of age'. The iron church, mentioned above, was situated on the site furthest from the photographer and was not removed until the main part of the new building had been completed. *(George Hobbs)*

Interior of St Alban's, 1935. Mr Marshall suggested using materials from Cheam Court Farm and he and Edward Swann were appointed joint architects. St Alban's is often called the 'barn church', not because it is a converted barn, but because the nave, seen here, was constructed from the timbers of two of the larger barns and the aisles from the cowsheds. One of the smaller barns made up the front of the organ chamber while a Jacobean floor became the ceiling of the vestry. Even the font is recycled: it was the font from the old St Dunstan's Church which was demolished in 1864 (see page 44). The structure has changed very little inside, and is still delightful. *(Lilian Curd)*

Part of the pageant 'The Church's Year' performed in the garden of Cheam Rectory, Malden Road, *c.* 1920. The leader of the pageant was the Revd Richard Wheeler who became the vicar of St John's Belmont from 1925 to 1959. Standing, left to right are Miss Parkin, Miss Hester Wesley-Dennis, Miss Bacon, Miss Ainsworth and Miss Braby. Kneeling in the centre is Lilian Mitchell (now Lilian Curd). Just visible through the trees is Cheam Baptist Church. *(Lilian Curd)*

Cheam School chapel, *c.* 1930. For 215 years Cheam School occupied the site at the top of Cheam High Street, where Tabor Court now stands. Founded by 1645, the school claims to be the oldest private school in the country and its chapel was widely considered to be the finest private chapel in Surrey. When encroaching development made movement to the country more and more desirable, the headmaster, the Revd Harold Taylor, mooted the idea of raising funds to finance the chapel's bodily removal to the school's new home near Newbury. A last reunion of old boys took place during 1934, prior to the school's move, and chapel bricks were 'auctioned' to raise funds. The first brick was purchased by Lord Mersey for £50. I wonder if Lord Mersey was refunded his 'brick' money when the plan to move the chapel fell through? (*Author's Collection*)

St Christopher's Roman Catholic Church, 20 March 2003. Cheam School Chapel was built at very much at the same time as the new St Dunstan's Church – the church being completed in 1864, the chapel in 1867. After the school left Cheam, in 1934, the ex-school chapel became a Roman Catholic church. Since then the congregation has extended their church to the south-west (the new entrance can be seen on the left) and has also added parish offices around the former apse. (*George Hobbs*)

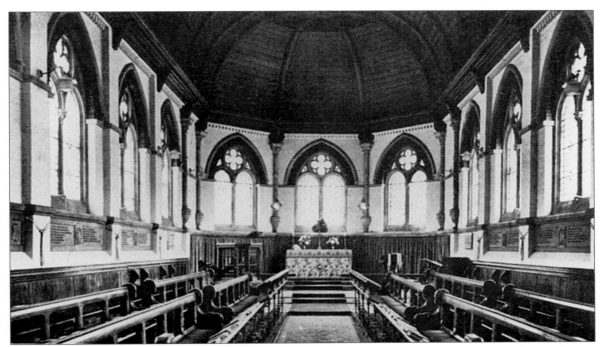

Interior, Cheam School Chapel, *c.* 1930. The chapel was built by Robert Tabor, as part of an extensive programme to enlarge the school. His sons, including Arthur who was later to succeed him as headmaster, plus several other boys boarded at Whitehall (see page 11) while the building work was going on. The dedication service for the chapel was to have been taken by the archbishop of Canterbury, Dr Longley, who was a past pupil of Cheam, but he had to cancel. His place was taken by Dr Waldegrave, bishop of Carlisle. The two Tabors, father and son, are remembered in Tabor Gardens and Tabor Court, the road and block of flats which were built on the site of the school buildings after they were demolished. (*Courtesy The Thornhill Press*)

Interior, St Christopher's Roman Catholic Church, 14 June 2003. The most obvious change is the reorientation of the church through ninety degrees. The altar now faces a new nave created by removing part of the old west wall and extending the building westwards. The addition makes the church T-shaped, with the altar now in the middle of what was previously one of the side walls. The reorganisation not only means that everyone in the extended building is able to see the celebration, but also that the altar has resumed its traditional position at the east end of the church. (*George Hobbs*)

Cuddington Croft Primary School under construction, 20 May 1965. Cheam grew dramatically during the first third of the last century, as suburban streets and houses took the place of rural areas; the increase in traffic was one of the major reasons Cheam School moved further out. The influx of new residents, coupled with the general population growth in the 1960s, meant that new schools were needed. Cuddington Croft was, and indeed still is, an unusually large primary school with over 400 full-time pupils and about fifty part-time pupils in the nursery. (© *Carlton Contractors Ltd and courtesy of Cuddington Croft Primary School*)

Cuddington Croft Primary School under construction, 22 July 1965. Before the 1960s the 11+ examination was fundamental in deciding whether pupils would go to a grammar, secondary modern or technical school. At primary school children were taught the subjects necessary to pass the important examination. Bright children were often placed in a top 'stream' and English, mathematics and communication and reasoning were considered particularly important. (© *Carlton Contractors Ltd and courtesy of Cuddington Croft Primary School*)

Cuddington Croft Primary School under construction, 18 January 1966. During the 1960s there was a fundamental change in education. So-called 'progressive ideals' were introduced into primary schools and comprehensive schools replaced grammar schools in many areas, although not in Cheam. Corporal punishment became far less widely used and various innovative – some would even say 'barmy' – ideas for educating children were tried. As the 11+ examination became less important, primary schools became more flexible about what was taught, and how. (© *Carlton Contractors Ltd and courtesy of Cuddington Croft Primary School*)

Cuddington Croft Primary School, 20 March 2003. Outwardly the school buildings have changed remarkably little, with only the addition of a new reception office visible to the far right of the photograph. Today teaching is dominated by the national curriculum, and children are assessed at many stages. The thinking has come full circle though, as children are now encouraged to concentrate on English, mathematics and science. Information technology, however, was certainly not part of the 1950s curriculum. (*George Hobbs*)

Ambleside School, 5 October 2002. Ambleside School has been part of Cheam since 1926 and it was a sad day for the village when it closed at the end of term in July 2001. The pressures on schools to adhere to the national curriculum and conform with key level testing cannot have helped small independent schools to survive. A pity because the teaching at Ambleside was always excellent and the school had several famous former pupils, including the racing driver James Hunt. *(Author's collection)*

Ambleside Development, 1 West Drive, 24 May 2003. The old school buildings have been swept away and four- and five-bedroom houses have replaced them. To attract buyers and emphasise the quality of its development Silver Homes has installed state-of-the-art features, including 'wiring system for integral sound and vision system, including satellite points with capacity for distribution throughout. Wired for internet connexion in the principal rooms there is also CAT 5 cabling for internal network systems and MRS built-in sound system.' Whatever that means! Even though each of the properties has an asking price in the region of £750,000, by the time this book is published they may be occupied. *(George Hobbs)*

St Anthony's Hospital, 1904–14. Founded and still owned by the Daughters of the Cross in England, a Catholic order devoted to education, nursing and community care, St Anthony's Hospital has been a major factor in the community life of North Cheam for a hundred years. The hospital admitted its first patients, Mrs Hoskins and her four-year-old son, both suffering from tuberculosis, on 5 July 1904. The building was known as North Cheam House and had been the home of the Macaskie family, although then owned by Mr R.H. Burdett. Although a family dwelling when the Sisters bought it, the part of the building on the right with the dormer windows was originally the Lord Nelson coaching inn. The pub still exists, at least in name, about a quarter of a mile east along the London Road. *(Courtesy of St Anthony's Hospital)*

St Anthony's Hospital, *c.* 1953. With the original building proving far too small for the numbers of patients seeking care, the Sisters set about organising the building of a new hospital. Building began in early 1914 and the 100-bed hospital was completed just over a year later. Most of the early patients were soldiers from the First World War. The three bays at the front of the building had originally been balconies, on to which tubercular patients were wheeled to benefit from fresh air. In April 1953 the balconies were enclosed to provide more ward space, as can be seen in the photograph. *(Courtesy of St Anthony's Hospital)*

Aerial view looking north-west, St Anthony's Hospital and St Raphael's Hospice, 1988. The hospice is probably the most striking building in the photograph; it is roughly H-shaped with the light roof just below left of centre. In the centre of the photograph are the hospital buildings. The entrance to the hospital grounds is at the crossroads in the centre, where the busy London Road crosses the lower third of the picture. The first hospital building was situated very close to the road, just to the right of the current entrance, on what is now lawn. *(Courtesy of St Anthony's Hospital)*

The biggest change noticeable is the building of St Bede's conference centre, to the north west of St Raphael's Hospice (towards the bottom left corner). The single-storey conference centre was built during 1992–3 and replaced the prefabricated buildings on the same site. The hospital has a history of striving to improve conditions for the care of the sick, and since the earlier photograph was taken other significant changes have also taken place. St Raphael's has been extended to the north and south to house fourteen in-patients and provide office space for the growing home-care team. St Anthony's has been extended to the south east to incorporate a new eight-bed intensive care unit. A new operating theatre and a modern, stylish entrance porch have also been added. (**getmapping**)

St Anthony's Hospital operating theatre, 1915. Not the oldest of St Anthony's operating theatres, but possibly the most elegant. It might look like a Victorian conservatory but the glass walls and roof were strictly practical. Interior walls were covered with white tiles. The result was a brightly lit and easy-to-clean theatre. Mr Romanus, appointed visiting surgeon at the time, looked out of the windows of the theatre and commented memorably: 'Sister, I know that as a surgeon at this hospital I should not say as much, but it is a fact that all the paths in the grounds of this hospital seem to lead to the mortuary!' *(Courtesy of St Anthony's Hospital)*

St Anthony's Hospital, operating theatre, *c.* 1960. The hospital has always striven to adopt the most up-to-date medical practices. In world health circles the 1960s saw the introduction of transplant surgery, while the '70s saw the development of computerised axial tomography, better known as CAT scanning. Perhaps even more importantly, St Anthony's began to look more closely at the interrelated needs of the patient; medical treatment was, for the first time, considered as only one aspect – albeit a very important one – of care as a whole. *(Courtesy of St Anthony's Hospital)*

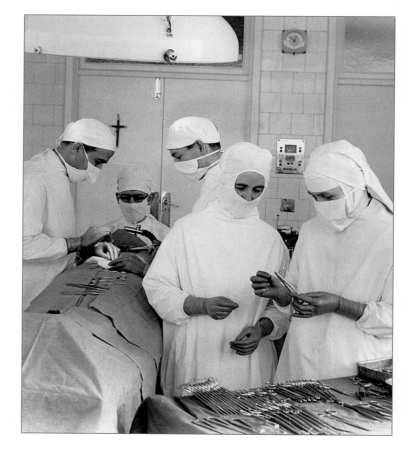

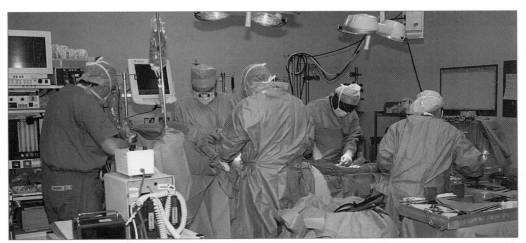

St Anthony's Hospital, operating theatre, 10 May 2001. Modern operating techniques include laparoscopic, better known as 'keyhole', surgery and the use of lasers. In this case E.E. John Smith is performing coronary artery bypass surgery. The surgical team is, left to right, Dr Bernie Liban (consultant anaesthetist), Mr Alex Melua (resident cardiac surgeon), Mr John Smith (consultant cardiothoracic surgeon), Dr Clement Akomea-Agyin (resident cardiac surgeon), Susie Downs (theatre nurse). Operations performed at St Anthony's range from simple procedures carried out on day patients under a local anaesthetic to complex major operations, including open heart surgery. *(Courtesy of St Anthony's Hospital)*

Nurse training, 1960s-style. Many of today's patients of St Anthony's Hospital don't realise that for many years the hospital ran a highly successful nurse training school. The school trained more than 1,600 nurses over forty years and remained open until 1972 when the Ministry of Health withdrew its support. Recently the hospital's contact with student nurses has been renewed as it once again provides clinical placements for nurse training. *(Courtesy of St Anthony's Hospital)*

Below: St Anthony's Hospital grounds, 1948. It was the custom at St Anthony's to hold occasional outdoor services to which locals, patients and their families were invited. A traditional part of the service was a procession around the ground by the off-duty nursing staff, sisters and others connected with the hospital. 1948 was the year the National Health Service was created and most hospitals in the country were taken into the scheme. St Anthony's, like other Catholic hospitals, was allowed to remain outside the scheme but offered beds for use by NHS patients. *(Courtesy of St Anthony's Hospital)*

Above: Some of the staff standing in front of St Anthony's Hospital, June 2003. With its need for nurses, doctors, auxiliary nursing staff, cleaners, caterers, administrators and gardeners, St Anthony's and St Raphael's are now the biggest employers in North Cheam. St Anthony's was granted the Investors in People award in 1996. The hospital also has a history of welcoming employees from other countries. In former years a large number of the nursing staff travelled from Ireland seeking employment and found their niche at the hospital. Today several of the highly skilled nursing staff come from the Philippines. Many local people spend much of their working life at the hospital and some local families have several members, often in different generations, working at St Anthony's; thirty years' service is not uncommon. Standing at the front of their dedicated staff are some of the nuns who are spiritual heirs to the sisters who started it all. Left to right: Sister Caroline, Sister Mary Geraldine, Sister Mary Damian, Sister Mary Declan and Sister Imelda. Sister Mary Damian is responsible for the nuns and ultimately responsible for the hospital and hospice; Sister Mary Geraldine will be familiar to many visitors to St Anthony's as a smiling face at the reception desk. *(Courtesy of St Anthony's Hospital)*

St Anthony's Hospital, 29 March 2003. The modern hospital, dating from 1975, opened a new era in the life of St Anthony's. Heavy investment in diagnostic facilities, including MRI and CT scanners, together with improved operating techniques and a shorter length of stay means that the hospital can treat many more patients. In recent years St Anthony's has renewed its ties with the NHS, helping to reduce waiting lists and providing clinical training places for student nurses. (*George Hobbs*)

St Raphael's Hospice, 29 March 2003. If St Anthony's was largely the work of the nuns, the hospice soon caught the imagination of the local community. Funds were raised through activities ranging from sponsored story writing by the pupils of St John Fisher Primary School to participation in the 1986 *Sunday Times* Fun Run by Sister Mary Perpetua and Sister Imelda. Even the workmen and subcontractors of the hospice's builders, John Laing Construction, got in on the act and raised over £16,000. On 21 April 1987 the hospice admitted its first patient, Mr Charles Barnes. Now over 2,000 patients per year benefit from the care the hospice provides. (*George Hobbs*)

3

Getting About

Old milestone, London Road, North Cheam, 21 April 2003. Milestones were essential when roads were few, travel dangerous and maps rare. The roads were the responsibility of the parish until turnpike trusts were established in the eighteenth and nineteenth centuries. Such trusts paid for the upkeep of the road by raising revenue from tolls levied on travellers. They also installed milestones and rudimentary signposts to ensure that their 'customers' didn't get lost. Deciding the exact age of this milestone would need an expert, but the style, a simple flat stone with an inscription which can be read from both directions, is old. *(George Hobbs)*

Not so long ago ordinary people were restricted in the distance they could travel by how far they could walk. People walked more then, of course, and would think nothing of walking several miles, but even so, neighbouring districts which we think of as being quite close would have been impossible for them to reach. Very few would have got even as far as Richmond or Reigate; London might as well have been the moon.

Travelling expectations changed, at least partially, in the middle of the nineteenth century. Trams, ubiquitous in the capital, never reached Cheam, but the railway was another matter. If the services of the water company opened up new areas for possible housing (see introduction to Chapter 1), the railway brought commuters to live in the new developments. When the London, Brighton and South Coast Railway laid the line through Cheam Village, North Cheam was little more than a crossroads with a couple of houses and a pub. It's one of the very few busy suburbs in the area still not served by a railway station. It has far fewer regular commuters than its older neighbour and has therefore become much more of a centre for retail and commerce in its own right.

The railway line through Cheam Village opened in 1847, *en route* to Epsom. Rather like today, many trains did not continue further west than Sutton and not all of the ones that did stopped at Cheam. (Very frustrating it is too.) Probably one of the most famous addresses in the area relates to the railway. Tony Hancock famously lived in Railway Cuttings, East Cheam, but fans trying to find it would be disappointed. Not only does it not exist, it's impossible; the railway line is on an embankment as it passes through Cheam.

In 1911 the line through Cheam was expanded from two to four tracks and a passenger subway with skylight lighting dug in preparation for an island platform which was never installed. The station was rebuilt and the booking office moved from the north to the south side in anticipation of an express service which didn't materialise. At the east end of the station a very long steel bridge replaced the single brick arch called Hales Bridge, after the local farmer who'd owned the land. In 1929 the steel bridge was itself replaced by the current concrete one and the former moved to Guildford and re-used as a footbridge. It was certainly still there a few years ago, seventy years later.

Cheam also had its own signal box. The first one was relatively small and situated at the end of the platform to the right of the door leading from the current booking hall. Its replacement was huge, extremely impressive and situated beyond the west end of the London platform and just east of the road going under the line. It was used from 1 October 1911 until 28 May 1978. After signalling was transferred to Victoria and the box closed the Bluebell Railway, a steam preservation line in Sussex, became interested in buying it. The Bluebell was actually negotiating the box's purchase when it was burnt down in an arson attack on 14 January 1983. Shame.

If geology has had a hand in shaping Cheam, so has transport – as much by where it's forbidden as by where permitted. North Cheam had fewer roads, but also fewer restrictions. Farms were in private ownership, common land not incommutable and development of roads and houses far less restricted. Cheam Village is bounded to the south by Cuddington and Banstead golf courses, the former of which was founded early in the twentieth century, effectively preventing much in the way of road development. The quiet roads in southern Cheam are excellent for more sedate motoring and a number of residents' own classic vehicles. The situation changes once motorists stray outside the quiet conclave next to the golf courses. The locals don't call that particular stretch of the A217 'the mad mile' because there used to be a lunatic asylum nearby, but because it's the only stretch between Cheam and the M25 without speed restrictions.

If the golf courses restricted road development to the south, Nonsuch Park prevented much expansion to the west. It's therefore somewhat ironic that unused roads appear on both green areas. Whenever there's an extended dry spell an old trackway becomes visible on Cuddington golf course, which runs across the second tee and seems to be part of a road joining Cheam Village to Banstead. Nonsuch Park, on the other hand, is home to two mile-long parallel concreted roads, now hidden by trees. They were apparently part of a by-pass to Worcester Park begun before the war, interrupted by hostilities and abandoned once the war had ended. The embryo road follows a lane shown on mid-nineteenth-century maps. Cheam's history would have been very different if a main road had been carved through the heart of Nonsuch. And while we're talking about lost lanes, people walking their dogs, joggers, or those merely wanting a short cut across the railway line are very pleased to find one just off the end of Bramley Road. The narrow archway cut through the railway embankment and emerging into Nonsuch Park was originally the entrance to Warren Farm, the house and yard of which lay about 50 yards on the north side of the railway embankment on the east of its access road.

Cheam is very fortunate in its network of foot and cycle paths and there is a strong cycling community in the area. St Christopher's Roman Catholic Church even has a memorial to the area's Catholic cyclists placed by the St Christopher's Catholic Cycling Club. Appropriate – St Christopher is, after all, the patron saint of travellers. Representatives from the local branch of the Cyclists' Touring Club frequently run guided cycle rides through Cheam and beyond. Those for beginners and families start in Nonsuch Park, those for experienced cyclists from North Cheam crossroads.

Our travelling habits have changed hugely since the days of carriages for the gentry and shanks's pony for the plebs. Nevertheless, caged in our cars away from the elements and each other, the roads along which we still journey have been shaped by different needs from our own. Transport has, indeed, come a long way.

Cheam station, 11 December 1981. This view is taken from the London end of the station and shows the old semaphore signals, which were controlled from a signal box out of sight at the far end of the station. The huge space visible between the two tracks had been occupied by two through loops on which fast expresses could pass stopping trains. The track was lifted in 1977–8, shortly before this shot was taken. The flats on the left are being constructed on the former goods yards. (*George Hobbs*)

Cheam station, 9 March 2003. Bushes have grown up beside the path and prevent photographs being taken from exactly the same spot as in the previous picture, but there are still a few changes. The flats have now matured and the semaphore signals were replaced in about 1983 with the almost universal red-green colour lights. The head of the light signal is in the same place as its semaphore predecessor and signalling is now controlled from Victoria. On the right a South Central train, in obsolete Connex livery, leaves the up platform *en route* for town. (*George Hobbs*)

No. 35028 *Clan Line* approaching Cheam. This could be a scene from the '60s but the photograph was in fact taken on 21 November 1998. The Merchant Navy class 4–6–2 locomotive was hauling the 'Solent & Sarum' charter train from Victoria to Southampton and Salisbury, passing through Cheam on its way. These locomotives were known as 'spam cans' because they were originally covered in a streamlined steel case. Such casing might have improved speed but made access for maintenance a nightmare and the streamlining was soon removed. *Clan Line* was one of the last two of its class to be modified and was rebuilt without casing in 1959. *(George Hobbs)*

The 455 electric train, photographed here on 9 March 2003, is a much more usual sight on the line through Cheam to Dorking or Guildford. Both this photograph and the previous one were taken from the long concrete bridge which spans Mulgrave Road, the railway line and the old goods yard, and which carries the Sutton by-pass. The bridge, built in 1929, is a very large reinforced concrete structure for the time. The photographs are unusual in that the bridge parapet is particularly high. Photographers must either be very tall, or carry something to stand on to be able to see the line. *(George Hobbs)*

Sutton to Wimbledon line, near West Sutton station, October 1987. Surrey was extremely badly affected by the hurricane which swept though southern England on the night of 14–15 October 1987. All the railway lines in the area were blocked with fallen debris and no traffic moved in or out of Cheam the following day. A massive clear up was put into effect and major routes were cleared quickly, but it took some weeks for normal service to be resumed. The wrong sort of leaves on the line indeed. *(Ron Taylor, Cheam Camera Club)*

Railway bridge, Burdon Lane, 8 February 2003. Painting the Forth Bridge must pale into insignificance compared with the task of maintaining hundreds of miles of railway infrastructure. There are actually two bridges at this point, the original brick-built structure and a girder bridge added beside the arch when the tracks were quadrupled in 1907. Engineers contracted to Network Rail routinely service the structures under its care and this was the turn of the bridge by the old forge. During one weekend they repaired brickwork, added reflective strips and good lighting and generally tidied up. The company might be good at mending bridges but it can't spell: each bridge has a designated name for easy identification. The sign under this one calls it 'Burden Lane'. Perhaps it is to them. Mind you, they have some excuse: depending on which map you use, the road here is labelled Burdon Lane, Sandy Lane or Station Way. *(George Hobbs)*

Kingsway terminus point at the rear of the Century Cinema, 18 July 1953. Who now remembers bus route 262? Probably not many because it lasted less than a year. The route was introduced on an experimental basis on 10 June 1953 to run up and down the hill between Cheam Village and Cuddington Way. A large detour, encompassing probably a third of the distance travelled, was necessary to cross the railway line by way of the Sutton by-pass as the bridge on the previous page is too low to allow a double-decker bus to pass. The bus is a very early post-war 'relaxed utility' body Daimler, fleet number D203. (© *Alan Cross*)

Colombo, Ceylon, *c.* 1955. From trundling up and down the quiet backwaters of Cheam, the Daimler D203 in the previous picture was shipped to Ceylon (now Sri Lanka) in December 1953. It became IC 2094 and started a new life trundling up and down the busy street of the island's main town. The South Western Omnibus Company (1952) Ltd of Ceylon wanted to increase its fleet and did so by buying second-hand London buses. The only obvious difference in the bus's appearance from its Cheam days is that its upper deck has twice as many opening windows. Perhaps Cheam isn't as warm as Colombo. (*Courtesy Capital Transport*)

Cuddington Down Side terminus, 18 July 1953. The route was designed to serve the residents of the estate of pre-fabs on Cuddington Way but consistently failed to pay its way. In spite of pleas from the Cuddington Way Residents' Association for its retention, the route was withdrawn on the evening of Tuesday 2 March 1954. This type of bus didn't even last that long and was withdrawn from service at the end of 1953. (© *Alan Cross*)

Sandy Lane, 14 June 2003. Almost exactly fifty years later, but the transport hasn't changed much. A few more houses appear in the background, but, because of the golf courses (see chapter introduction) traffic seldom disturbs this part of Cheam. Learner drivers love it! The car, a 1951 Vauxhall Wyvern, is owned by a local resident and has been in the same family since 1956. It was purchased second-hand in Gloucester, in part exchange for a 1951 650cc Triumph Thunderbird motorbike. (*George Hobbs*)

Kingsway terminus point at the rear of the
Century Cinema, 27 February 1954.
The 'relaxed utility' body Daimler bus
which operated the service for the last half
of 1953 has been replaced by an RT class
fleet number RT3718. As the route was
very short it only required one vehicle to
operate it and it was the bus pictured
which was used for the final run on
2 March 1954. It was a very cold evening
with hard snow still on the ground in
places. A small placard inscribed 'in
memory of the last 262' was tied to the
radiator with ribbon. (© Alan Cross)

Southern terminus point of the S7 route, 20 March 2003. The S7 was introduced on 16 November 2002
and runs from Anne Boleyn's Walk to Colliers Wood station, adjacent to the Merton garage of London
General. The southern terminus is near the rear entrance to the dairy (see page 23), the side wall of which
can be seen in the background. Drivers of the S7 route used to be allowed to share the dairy's staff facilities
when taking a break, but since its closure they have to make their own arrangements. The modern
terminus is about 200 yards from the 1954 terminus, across the car park directly behind the double-decker
in the top photograph. (George Hobbs)

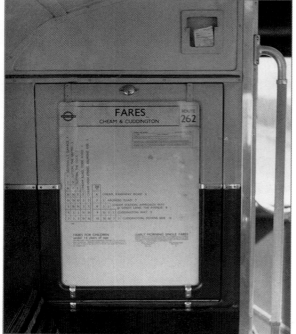

Interior showing the fares chart of RT registration NLE 825, fleet number RT3718, 27 February 1954. It is just possible to see that the fare from one end of the Cheam to Cuddington route to the other was 3½d. The bus stop fare stage names printed vertically on the left are the fares for travelling to or from Sutton Garage. This was in fact only possible once a day in each direction, when the bus was entering service and travelling from the garage and when it was returning home after the last timetabled run. The fare for the journey was 7d. (© Alan Cross)

Interior of Optare fleet number Op3, 20 March 2003. Fare boards are no longer displayed internally because of the wide variety of concessions available, but the bus company currently charges an adult rate of 70p inside the Greater London boundary, regardless of destination. The vehicles themselves are smaller, lower and seating is no longer of the bench variety. They also fit under bridges (see page 79). More subtle introductions, which are an unfortunate sign of the times, are CCTV cameras concealed at the back of the bus, in the two domes on the ceiling to the left and at certain points externally. Driver Gary Bishop (seated) explained that the cameras were to help ensure the safety of both passengers and staff. He also mentioned that they were useful when dealing with complaints about the non-arrival of the buses, as each camera recorded the time as well as internal/external view as appropriate. The buses are garaged at the Epsom depot in Longmead Road and, just as in 1954, must travel to and from their route each day. Unlike in 1954, Epsom Buses (Quality Line) does not carry passengers to and from Longmead Road, even once a day, so this mileage generates no revenue. Such an arrangement may soon change, however. At the time of writing there is a proposal to extend the S7 route as far as Epsom and to withdraw the 408. (George Hobbs)

4

Getting Together

Cheam Camera Club, Epsom, 1988. Members of the Cheam Camera Club must be pretty good as it won the *Surrey Advertiser* Rosebowl Challenge for 2003. The club, a member of the Surrey Photographic Association, meets on Wednesdays at the Tweddle Hall (see page 50) and organises guest speakers and visits offering the opportunity to practise and develop photographic skills. Standing up to their chins in rushes at the edge of a pond is obviously such an event. I wonder what they're all looking at? Newcomers are always welcome! They always say that a good photographer takes pictures of things other people miss.
(Ron Taylor, Cheam Camera Club)

When people first gathered in one place to live it can't have been long before they decided to give their place a name. Cheam has had about a dozen different names, all variations of each other. Most people at the time couldn't read or write, and there was no formal spelling, so passing down names became like a giant game of Chinese whispers – medieval text messaging, if you like. In 967 the area was called Cegham; just over a century later in 1086, when the Domesday Book was compiled, the name had transmuted to Ceiham. Yet another variation in spelling, Cheyham, still exists in some of the road names in Cheam Village. The name probably means 'homestead or village by the tree stumps' from the Old English words *ham*, meaning a village and *ceg*, meaning a stump. Our word 'keg' today is derived from the same root: a barrel looks a little like a tree stump.

Names are important because they are usually a mini-description. Such is true for people as well as places. A former pupil of Cheam School is Admiral the Honourable Sir Reginald Aylmer Ranfurly Ernle-Erle-Drax-Plunkett. The admiral's name alone tells us a good deal about him and the history of his family. In a similar way, 'Ceiham' tells us firstly that the place held a sizable community for the time. The Domesday Book indicates that the village probably consisted of about 150 people plus seventeen heavy wooden ploughs, each of which would have been pulled by a team of four to six oxen. The second fact revealed by the name is that it was in an area which had once been wooded but which had been cleared for farmland, which in turn suggests a feeling of community and people used to helping each other.

Living in a relatively isolated area at the foot of the desolate North Downs bequeathed the people of Cheam a sense of mutual self-help which lingers to this day. There are a large number of semi-formal clubs, societies, groups and organisations, and informal gatherings spring up for particular events or as the need arises. During the war a youth club was organised for evacuees in a garden in Cuddington Way. In 2002 the residents of The Glade arranged a spectacular street party to celebrate the Golden Jubilee. Nearly sixty years ago local newly married couples were experiencing difficulty getting somewhere to live after the war. They had a licence to build but there was a long wait for labour and materials and the licence would have lapsed if nothing had been done. Fathers, brothers, uncles and neighbours got together to dig foundations and some locals are still living in the house their family helped to build.

Of course, such communities produce characters. During the '50s 'the Major' lived in West Drive and was a great man for the ladies; he disappeared, owing money everywhere. Sergeant Yeomans was a Chelsea pensioner with a French wife and used to man the gate to Nonsuch Park in the early part of the twentieth century. A well-known local character of rather longer ago was Dr William Gilpin, headmaster of Cheam School from 1752 to 1777. He was a famous art critic, wrote several books of tours and virtually invented the idea of the picturesque. His ideas were parodied by, among others, Jane Austen: 'I have no knowledge in the picturesque . . . I shall call hills steep, which ought to be bold; surfaces strange and uncouth, which ought to be irregular and rugged'. (Edward Ferrars, chapter 18, *Sense and Sensibility*). Gilpin was thinly disguised as Dr Syntax in Thomas Rowlandson's pictures and William Combe's verse. He was also the model for Mr Jennings, schoolmaster in Tobias Smollett's *Peregrine Pickle*.

As well as individualists, Cheam has had its fair share of the rich and famous. Most know of the two Harrys who lived in Cheam, VIII and Secombe, and also that it was the fictional residence of Tony Hancock (it was actually Hancock's first agent Phyllis Rounce who lived in Cheam. The writers, Alan Simpson and Ray Galton, thought it such a funny name they adopted it). Fewer know about Cheam's other famous residents. Elizabeth I retreated to Nonsuch Palace away from the threat of the Armada. Lord Randolph Churchill, father of Sir Winston, was a pupil of Cheam School, as was His Royal Highness The Duke of Edinburgh. Prince Philip's son, Prince Charles, also attended Cheam School, but that was after it had moved to near Newbury. I wonder whether they compared notes? George V and Queen Mary knew Cheam, too; they had been visitors to Nonsuch Manor. Other famous former residents include Petula Clarke in North Cheam, David Bellamy in Stoughton Avenue, Michael Aspel in Chatsworth Road and Edwin Landseer, who lived where Landseer Road is now.

Celebrities are all very well, but it's the ordinary people, living and working in the area, who make a community. Because of the lack of water (see introduction to chapter 1) agricultural land in Cheam was relatively poor, so Cheam became a small centre for craftworkers – appropriate for a community whose parish church is dedicated to St Dunstan (see page 44). In the late Middle Ages the area was known for its potteries, and particularly for its jug making. London clay, on which the north part of Cheam is built, and which makes good earthenware pots, was almost certainly the reason for the existence of the cottage industry. The remains of two kilns have been discovered, one in the High Street dating from around 1500, and the other in Park Side from the fourteenth century and on the site of what used to be Cheam House. The potteries continued until about 1650, although with a much lower output. They probably did not produce fancy enough ware for Elizabeth I to have used when she visited Nonsuch Palace, but her servants would have been familiar with Cheam pottery.

Pottery no longer appears to be practised to any extent in Cheam, but ancient skills are still kept alive by the Cheam Woodturners Association, whose members produce beautiful and useful items using age-old techniques. Cheam as a community is alive and well, with organisations including residents' associations, Friends of Whitehall, several Guide companies and Brownie packs, Sutton and Cheam Radio Society, Friends of Cheam Park and Cheam Recreation Ground, Boys Brigade, Cheam Camera Club, Sutton and Cheam Society, Nonsuch Antiquarian Society, North Cheam Sequence Dance. . . .

Cheam Home Guard, *c.* 1943. The photograph is taken on the Sutton and Epsom Rugby Club ground behind Northey Avenue. Originally called the Local Defence Volunteers, the Home Guard was made up of men in reserved occupations or who were too old for active service. It became known affectionately as 'Dad's army'. The names of most of this group are unknown, but Mr Charles Turner is seated in the centre. He was a gunner instructor and lived in Hay's Walk. Can anyone explain why the gentleman on his right is apparently parading with a walking stick? *(Muriel Reed)*

Farringdon House, London Road, 5 April 2003. North Cheam is still home to army volunteers as 151 Logistic Support Regiment, Royal Logistic Corps (Volunteers) is based at the Territorial Army Centre at Farringdon House. The RLC, both Regular and Territorial Army, was formed on 5 April 1993 from the Royal Army Ordnance Corps, the Royal Corps of Transport, the Army Catering Corps, the Royal Pioneer Corps and the Corps of Royal Engineers (Postal and Courier Branch): the Ministry of Defence decided that boots, grub and letters should all be handled by the same organisation. *(George Hobbs)*

Rugby ground between Cheam Road and Northey Avenue, 1940. During one of the air raids which pounded the area a stick of three bombs fell in the rugby ground off Cheam Road. The middle one exploded and blew up the pavilion, but the other two were dealt with by a bomb disposal team, whose lorry is pictured. Here the local Home Guard examines one of the bombs after it has been made safe (one hopes). *(Muriel Reed)*

Sutton and Epsom Rugby Club ground, 20 March 2003. Perhaps surprisingly in an area where housing in-fill is common, the rugby club ground is still enjoyed as an open space. The grounds themselves look much as they did in 1940, although the stand and mobile phone mast are, of course, much more recent. In May 1998 property developers proposed to build fifty-five houses on the site but were defeated in a High Court judgement when residents, supported by the Cheam Neighbourhood Action Group, objected. The Lord of the Manor of Ewell discovered restrictive covenants written by his ancestors which protect the playing fields for the local use. *(George Hobbs)*

Field Day Communications, late 1940s. After the war radio amateurs were encouraged to operate under emergency conditions as a means of keeping communications open in times of crisis. A like-minded group of the Radio Society of Great Britain (RSGB) members met in Ye Olde Red Lion in Cheam Village on 1 October 1946. The group subsequently formed into the Sutton and Cheam Radio Society on 20 May 1947. Here Stan Vanstone (G2AYC) with the pipe and A.E. 'Mitch' Mitchell (G8DF) call radio 'hams' around the world using state-of-the-art equipment – for the time. *(Courtesy of Sutton and Cheam Radio Society)*

Above: Legal and General Sports Ground, Kingswood, 1981. The equipment is more up to date, but the tent is the same! Les Seaton (G3HSK) with the cap and Mike Pharaoh (G3LCH), the society's chairman at the time, concentrate on an incoming contact. Each amateur operator has a unique call sign with which to identify him- or herself on the air. The letter at the beginning of the call sign indicates the country in which the operator is licensed: British call signs begin with G or M, Indian ones with VU, etc. *(Courtesy of Sutton and Cheam Radio Society)*

Sutton and Cheam Radio Society, 1948. Amateur radio operators demonstrate their skills 'in the field' – often taken literally as here at Decca (later Racal) Sports' Ground. Note the gentleman at the top! It's impossible to be sure now, but it could be Jack Harris (G2BOF). The society's minute book records that the mast and aerial was built and erected by Stan Vanstone (G2AYC) (see pages 78–9). *(Courtesy of Sutton and Cheam Radio Society)*

Below: Sutton and Cheam Radio Society, 1948. Back on the ground again Jack Harris (G2BOF) checks the compass to ensure that it's accurately indicating the direction of the aerial. The aerial was rotated by hand using the rod and gearbox shown on the right of the photograph. 'Hams' are a highly skilled pool of technically trained people who are frequently called on to assist when normal communications are disrupted. In 1912, for example, one of the first people to intercept the distress signals of the *Titanic* was an amateur operator in Herefordshire called George Leadbetter. More recently numerous radio amateurs assisted with communications in New York following the Twin Towers disaster in September 2001. *(Courtesy of Sutton and Cheam Radio Society)*

Courtlands Farm, Banstead, 1985. Erecting the mast is something of a challenge but practice makes perfect. On mast-lifting duties are, left to right, Vic Harris (G1LKM), Paul Hughes (G0BXC) and Jack Korndorffer (G2DMR). Aluminium tubing and lightweight materials have replaced the wooden 'telegraph-style' pole, but the principle remains the same. Properly erected a mast can easily withstand winds of over 60 mph. *(Courtesy of Sutton and Cheam Radio Society)*

Courtland's Farm, Banstead, 1994. With the advent of increasingly portable equipment, the tent has been swapped for Pat Davenport's (G0GZQ) landrover, but the mast is still about 30 ft high. Many people fail to appreciate the expertise of radio 'hams' and their ability to communicate on a par with all sorts of radio operators around the world. Each enthusiast must pass a test to obtain an amateur transmitting licence before being issued with their own call sign. Licences are issued at three levels: foundation, which was introduced in January 2002 and is designed to get newcomers involved as quickly as possible, intermediate and full. For the upper two levels amateur operators must take the internationally recognised Radio Amateurs Examination (RAE) which includes the ability to send and receive Morse code at five words per minute. *(Courtesy of Sutton and Cheam Radio Society)*

Sutton Public Hall, 12 October 1949. Sutton and Cheam Radio Society at the Hobbies Exhibition run by the Rotary Club. The mayor and mayoress of Sutton and Cheam opened the transmitting station G4DH/A by broadcasting a message to Roy Scott (G2CZH) at Seymour Avenue, Morden Park. Left to right: a member of the hall management or mayoral party, Mrs Milne, Alderman W.D. Milne, Stan Vanstone (G2AYC). According to the *Sutton and Cheam Herald* the stand was 'perhaps the most spectacular show in the whole exhibition'. *(Courtesy of Sutton and Cheam Radio Society)*

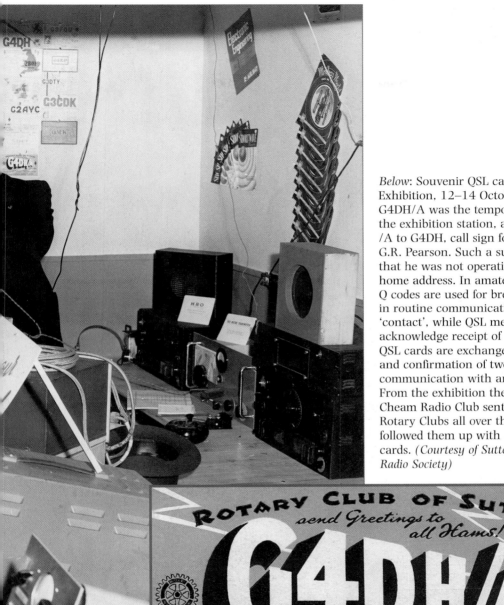

Below: Souvenir QSL card from Hobbies Exhibition, 12–14 October 1949. G4DH/A was the temporary call sign for the exhibition station, adding a suffix /A to G4DH, call sign for club member G.R. Pearson. Such a suffix indicates that he was not operating from his home address. In amateur radio circles Q codes are used for brevity and clarity in routine communication. QSO means 'contact', while QSL means 'I acknowledge receipt of transmission'; QSL cards are exchanged as a courtesy and confirmation of two-way communication with another 'ham'. From the exhibition the Sutton and Cheam Radio Club sent greetings to Rotary Clubs all over the world and followed them up with appropriate QSL cards. *(Courtesy of Sutton and Cheam Radio Society)*

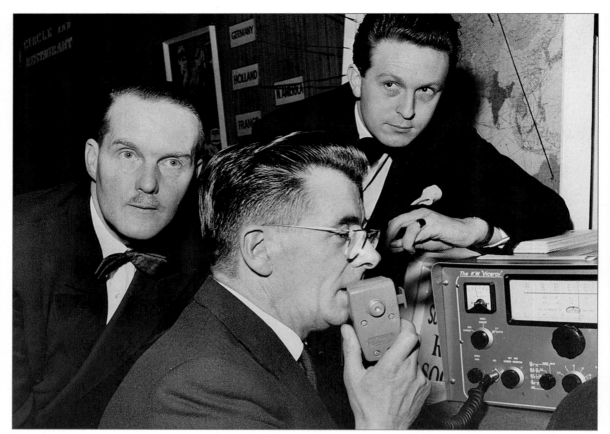

'Bob' Tillin (G3MES), Granada Cinema, Sutton, 20–24 December 1965. The minute book for the Sutton and Cheam Radio Society comments: 'at the request of the manager of the Granada Cinema, Sutton, a SSB [Single Side Band] station using the special call GB3SAC was established in the foyer.' Mr Tillin is demonstrating the skills of the amateur radio enthusiast using equipment, counted as portable at the time, to two well-known film and TV actors. (*'Bob' Tillin*)

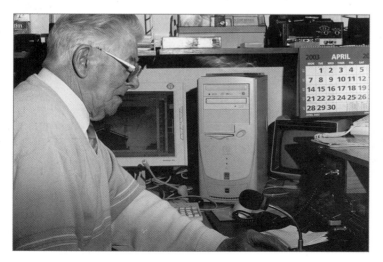

'Bob' Tillin (G3MES) transmitting from his home, 12 April 2003. 'Bob' joined the Sutton and Cheam Radio Society in 1956 and has seen a lot of changes. The KW Viceroy transmitter used at the Granada cinema, probably weighed half a hundredweight and consisted entirely of valves. Modern portable transceivers are totally transistorised with modern integrated circuits and can weigh less than a bag of sugar. (*George Hobbs*)

British Legion Parade along Northey Avenue, 22 April 1951. The British Legion, now the Royal British Legion, was formed in 1921. In 1951 two years National Service, later reduced to eighteen months, was still required of young men. The parade began with a short service in St Andrew's Church, and was led by the Mayor of Sutton and Cheam, Councillor Miss Dorothy Webster J.P. (*Courtesy of St Andrew's Church*)

Boys Brigade, Cheam Baptist Church, The Broadway, 1977. Founded in 1883 – about twenty-five years before the Scout movement – the Boys Brigade is the oldest uniform association for boys in the world. The Brigade's founder, William Smith, planned a programme which combined gymnastics, sport, drill and religious instruction. Today both boys and girls enjoy activities such as orienteering, skiing and canoeing. (*Ron Taylor, Cheam Camera Club*)

Air Raid Precautions (ARP) wardens' post number 34 in 1940. Post 34 was just opposite the entrance to the Sutton Rugby Club in Cheam Road. Muriel, known as 'Jo', Turner, now Muriel Reed, demonstrates the use of a stirrup pump while Margaret Woolston watches from the doorway. *(Muriel Reed)*

Cheam Road, 14 June 2003. ARP post 34 no longer exists, but Mrs Reed gallantly poses – plus stirrup pump – on the site where it was. As Margaret Woolston wasn't available, Joan Barratt kindly stands in as second in command. Passing motorists were fascinated! *(George Hobbs)*

5

Playing the Game

Pavilion, Cheam Sports Club, 1980. Opened on 2 October 1931, the pavilion saw in the club's diamond jubilee before being replaced by more modern and spacious buildings in April 2001. Tucked out of the way beyond the railway end of The Broadway, the history of the sports club has mirrored the UK's social and economic history since the middle of the nineteenth century. *(Courtesy Cheam Sports Club)*

For non-professionals sport is a leisure activity, and until recently leisure was relatively rare for ordinary people. In previous centuries, however, sport provided a training ground for hunting and war. At a time when the English longbow was a weapon of mass destruction, every village had by law to ensure that its menfolk practised regularly at the archery butts. Village women were neither expected to fight nor to hunt for food, but archery became a favoured pastime with great ladies. Queen Elizabeth's Elm stood very close to the public footpath north of the long ditch in Nonsuch Park until early in the twentieth century. When she stayed at Nonsuch she was said to stand by the huge tree and shoot deer with a crossbow.

'Enjoying good sport' almost always meant hunting, but that didn't mean that there were no rules. Rather as with game birds on moorland today, Cheam's warren (see introduction and page 25) provided a safe area for hares to breed. The hare wall was built partly to keep the hares in, and partly to keep the local poachers out. Dogs owned by the peasantry near the areas reserved for the king to hunt had to be proven unfit for chasing game. Very small dogs, measured by making the animal pass through a tiny hoop, were acceptable. Otherwise the dog had to be 'lawed', which meant removing two or three of the middle toes on its front feet to ensure that it could not run fast.

Falconry was another sport popular both with those who enjoyed the thrill of the chase and with those looking to catch their dinner. Social hierarchy was reflected in the type of birds flown: only the king could fly the gyrfalcon, while lords, including bishops, were allowed peregrine falcons. The merlin was a lady's bird, while young men could fly the hobby. A yeoman was allowed to fly a goshawk, the parish priest a sparrowhawk and the knave or serf had to make do with a kestrel.

Sport may have acted as a training ground but it was also good exercise. Henry VIII is known for being very fond of real tennis, and he and his father, Henry VII, built a number of courts across the country. There is no record of a real tennis court at Nonsuch but the wilderness, situated about a third of a mile to the west of the palace, was said to be adapted for court tennis, as the sport is known in the US. A Swiss visitor to Nonsuch, Thomas Platter, wrote in 1599 that 'a great many trees are uprooted and cleared, within a breadth of some eighteen to twenty feet, along a straight course. . . . And here and there they are partitioned off on either side with high boards, so that the balls may be played in the shade of these same alleys very pleasantly, as in an enclosed tennis court' (Clare Williams' translation). Each real tennis court may be slightly different, but the game is usually played on an enclosed area approximately 110 ft x 40 ft x 30 ft high. If Platter was describing a real tennis game he was either bad at judging distances or the court was very small indeed.

There is no doubt about the bowling green at the northern end of Nonsuch Palace, just in front of the main gate house. A survey in 1650 of Palace and Park states that 'about 8 yardes distance from the [palace] is a neate and hansome bouling greene well ordered' (sic), presumably the forerunner of the front lawn of a semi. Henry VIII was something of a spoilsport though: he banned those who were not wealthy from playing bowls because 'bowyers, fletchers, stringers and arrowhead makers' were spending more time playing than working.

Most sports have a much older history than we realise. James I, for example, in his publication *The Book of Sports*, condemned football and golf but encouraged bowls. He also formalised horse racing and instructed his son to exercise by 'running, leaping, wrestling, fencing, dauncing and playing at caitche or tennise' (sic). So much for jogging being thought a modern pastime. James would have approved of Cheam since the area has plenty of sports facilities. Cheam Sports Club and Cannons Leisure Centre in Peaches Close, the North Cheam Sports and Social Club, the David Lloyd Leisure Centre attached to Nonsuch School, Cuddington Golf Club, Cheam Leisure Centre in Malden Road, Cheam Recreation Ground, the old London Transport Executive Sports' Ground (see pages 36–7), the list goes on and on.

Not only does the area have a remarkable number of organised clubs and teams, but there are lots of facilities for less formal competition. A glance at a map of the area reveals a number of individual or small groups of tennis courts dotted about behind various back gardens and owned by small clubs or groups of people who enjoy getting together to play a friendly game. The same map may show the startling growth in back-garden swimming pools which, if hardly to Olympic standard, demonstrate their owners' enjoyment of air and exercise.

Many of the sports grounds in Cheam have interesting histories. In the latter part of the nineteenth century, Cheam cricket club rented various meadows on which to play, before leasing 5 acres of the grounds of Cheam House in 1875. Its owner, Spencer Wilde, also gave the land for the parish rooms and built the church's lych gate to celebrate his silver wedding anniversary. The land at Peaches Close was acquired in various parcels by Edward Boniface and leased to the sports club in 1919 with an option to buy. Two years later, on 9 November 1921, the club passed the resolution to do so.

Sports clubs also took over a couple of farms as being suitable open ground. The Sutton and East Ewell Rugby Ground is built on the site of Manor Farm; maps dating from around 1870 show a building on the raised area to the south. The same maps show that Cuddington Recreation Ground in North Cheam is on the site of Sparrow Farm, so called because it was owned by Mr Sparrow. Appropriately, the entrance to the recreation ground is off Sparrow Farm Road.

'Sport' comes originally from the fifteenth-century word 'disport', meaning to enjoy oneself or have fun. Whether it's archery or yoga, things haven't changed so much in five hundred years.

First page of the Cheam Cricket Club minute book, 1864. On 4 July of that year a group of cricket enthusiasts held a general meeting and established Cheam Cricket Club. Initially the club rented land on which to play and in 1875 5 acres of Cheam Park was leased from Spencer Wilde of Cheam House, one-time chairman of the club. By 1879 ladies were allowed to play tennis on part of the ground and in 1881 'cricket for boys' was introduced, possibly one of the earliest examples of colts' cricket. Records seem to have lapsed after 1889 but on 29 November 1919 some members met and were instrumental in establishing the Cheam Cricket and Sports Club. It has always been a matter for conjecture as to whether the newly titled club was a reformation of the original club or entirely new one. Certain it is that on 9 November 1921 the decision was taken to purchase the ground which now makes up the sports facilities on the north side of Peaches Close. *(Courtesy Cheam Sports Club)*

Cricket team, 1962. A comparison with the 1902 team opposite seems to show that the modern team has dispensed with the use of a bat, so it's just as well that their legs are far better protected. Standing, left to right: Tim Connolly, Roger Phillips, Jon Collier, Alan Coysh, Alan Agland, Tony Brown, Alan Perry, Basil Royle, Vernon Butcher, Mike Willoughby. Lying: David Morgan, Harold Smith. Around this time Cheam Cricket Club went through what is known as the Benefit Years when cricket matches were organised at Peaches Close between a Surrey XI and a celebrity or Cheam XI. Funds thus raised were given to a named Surrey player. Beneficiaries included Surrey's David Fletcher (1957), himself a Cheam member, Eric Bedser (1958), Bernie Constable (1959) and Peter Loader (1963). Following the success of the benefit matches, in 1968 Cheam was asked to stage an 'International Cavaliers' cricket match with John Edrich as beneficiary. BBC2 televised the event in colour – almost unheard of for the time – and a record attendance of 8,000 packed Peaches Close to watch players like Gary Sobers, Ted Dexter and Trevor Bailey. *(Courtesy Cheam Sports Club)*

Opposite: Cricket team, 1902. The earliest reference to sport being played at Peaches Close was the cricket of 1864, in days when Gentlemen versus Players was the norm and traditions were being laid down. Some obviously realised that white is one of the most impractical colours to wear for any sport, although it might be cooler in the heat of the summer. This team photo makes a startling fashion statement for the times. Facial hair and caps seem to have been the order of the day, although the vast array of different ties being worn to keep their whites up may disappoint many traditionalists. The names of this team have largely disappeared into the mists of time but Mr Ockenden, second from the right in the back row, is the son of a founder member. *(Courtesy Cheam Sports Club)*

Cricket Club dinner, 1956. Attended by more than 100 men – not being an age of equality, ladies were banned – the turnout is remarkable for a club made up of four teams of eleven. The numbers are testimony to the support Cheam Sports Club received and still continues to receive. The social side of all the sports played at Peaches Close is an integral part of every section that makes up the club. Each team plays competitively, but after the competition is over sport is a very social pastime. Amazingly each individual's face is visible here, each one atop a dark suit, often with the *de rigueur* handkerchief in the top pocket. The photograph probably took some time to set up and must have been taken before the meal: this can be the only explanation for the sobriety of the subjects and the lack of wine or beer on the tables. 1 Jack Connolly, 2 Female – banned!, 3 Mike Connolly, 4 Tim Connolly, 5 Peter Phillips, 6 -?-, 7 -?-, 8 -?-, 9 -?-, 10 -?-, 11 Bob Blake, 12 -?-, 13 Jack McCarthy, 14 Sid Harris, 15 Mike Higgins, 16 Walter Kirton,

17 David Morgan, 18 -?-, 19 -?-, 20 Eddie Boylan, 21 -?-, 22 -?-, 23 Bill Smith, 24 -?-, 25 Charlie Moxon, 26 -?-, 27 -?-, 28 -?-, 29 -?-, 30 Don Fisher, 31 Tony Cooke, 32 Bert Lawrence, 33 -?-, 34 Alan Agland, 35 Bill Cooper, 36 Johnny Ansell, 37 -?-, 38 Graham Fyson, 39 Dennis Rozier, 40 Edgar Jenkin, 41 Cliff Edwards, 42 Gilbert Corke, 43 -?-, 44 Darrel Fyson, 45 Clem Lee, 46 -?-, 47 Bruce Cowles, 48 Johnny Cripps, 49 Jack Mackins, 50 -?-, 51 Freddie Robson, 52 ? Jim Laker, 53 Basil Royle, 54 Stuart Surridge, 55 Ron Yapp, 56 Herbert Bligh, 57 Bob Bellfield, 58 -?-, 59 Ted Mason, 60 -?-, 61 -?-, 62 -?-, 63 -?-, 64 -?-, 65 -?-, 66 -?-, 67 Arthur Howell, 68 John Potter, 69 -?-, 70 -?-, 71 -?-, 72 -?-, 73 -?-, 74 -?-, 75 George Spear, 76 Edgar Truman, 77 -?-, 78 -?-, 79 -?-, 80 'Batch' Batchelor, 81 -?-, 82 -?-, 83 Jeff Jeffries, 84 Wally Veasey, 85 -?-, 86 Frank Kibble, 87 -?-, 88 -?-, 89 -?-, 90 ? Young, 91 -?-, 92 -?-, 93 -?-, 94 -?-, 95 Bill Gosden, 96 Bill Wycherley, 97 -?-, 98 -?-, 99 Laurie Pooley, 100 Frank Martin, 101 -?-, 102 -?-, 103 -?-, 104 -?-, 105 ? Thornby (brother of no. 107), 106 ? Thornby (father of nos 105 & 107), 107 Ted Thornby, 108 Alan Foley, 109 'Pritz', 110 Ralph Glover, 111 -?-. *(Courtesy Cheam Sports Club)*

Aerial view, Cheam Sports Club grounds, *c.* 1970. Seen from the air it becomes obvious how Cheam Sports Club dominates the local landscape. Bordered by the railway line to the north, successful design and planning maintains the fine balance between the needs of the local residents and those of the playing members. The vast size of the playing area – almost 13 acres – has allowed Peaches Close to play host to numerous sports over the years. Cricket, hockey, tennis, bowls, squash, korfball, karate and football, among others, are all played here and all benefit from the facilities at Peaches Close. Members have represented the sports club at a higher and, in some cases, international level. *(Courtesy Cheam Sports Club)*

Bedser XI vs. Cheam XI, 1962. As a friendly, the game was played with the emphasis very much on entertaining the crowd. Left to right: Charlie Moxham (umpire), Alan Agland, David Morgan, P.B.H. May, Ross Endean, Doug Ryder, Jon Hutchins, Mike Osborne. David Morgan, now the Sports Club archivist, took five wickets (unsurprisingly), although South African international Ross Endean seemed to pick the flight of this one quite nicely. The crowd at the far end are sitting in front of some of the fifty-two poplar trees donated by members at the beginning of the twentieth century. The trees are planted in front of the railway line and every one was watered in with half a pint of bitter, a tradition which still greets new club members to this day! Thirty of the poplars still survive and are one of the outstanding features of the ground. The other is the 120 ft sightscreen which was originally erected to hide building works on the other side of the railway. It is believed to be the second longest in the world, the crown going to one in Australia. (Courtesy Cheam Sports Club)

Scorecard, Festival Cricket Match, 1962. Surrey and England's Alec Bedser brought a star-studded team to Peaches Close to raise funds for the club. The stars had to rely on fielding twelve players, including seven internationals, to defeat a Cheam XI skippered by Harold Smith, at the time the club's youngest ever captain at twenty-four. Alec Bedser's original squad called on a certain Harry Secombe, singer, comedian, Goon, late order batsman and local resident. David Fletcher, the home team's number three, played for Surrey for many years and remained loyal to Cheam throughout this time. He managed several successful Surrey Young Cricketers teams which included many of the present county players such as Mark Butcher and Alistair Brown, thus maintaining the connection between Cheam colts' cricket and Surrey County Cricket Club.
(Courtesy Cheam Sports Club)

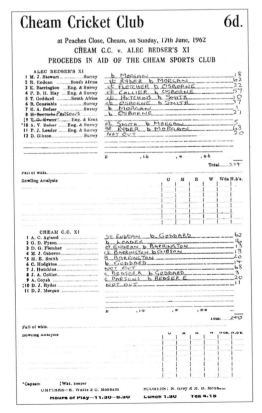

Cheam Cricket Team, national club cricket championship finalists, Lord's, 1990. Back row, left to right: Steve Want, Sean Travers, Chris Cornell, Gary Martin, Neil Driscoll, Peter James, Mike Witcomb (scorer). Front row: Mark Rowland, Dave Allen, Bob Falconer (captain), Andy Smith, David Morgan, Mark Butcher. 1990 was Cheam Cricket Club's most glorious summer and had been building for some time beforehand. A mix of youth and experience and a tremendous team spirit all came to fruition during one superb season. The team itself included a couple of generations of Cheam-bred cricketers such as Alistair Brown (not in the photograph because he had played too many limited overs matches for Surrey) and Mark Butcher, who went on to represent their country and was led from the front by Bob Falconer in his first season as captain.

Cheam had already won the Surrey Championship for the first time and were runners up to Blackpool in a memorable final at Lord's. The semi-final victory over Truro will live in the memory of everyone who watched it, as much for the style of victory as the atmosphere, with a huge crowd, barbecues around the boundary and bright sunshine – a great cricketing summer.
(Courtesy Cheam Sports Club)

Singles tennis championships, *c.* 1980. Left to right: -?-, -?-, Pat Proctor, -?-, Zenan Schram. During 1978 the tennis section visited Luxembourg and the following year returned the hospitality by welcoming members from the Spora Club to Cheam during Wimbledon fortnight. Any visitor to Cheam Sports Club is immediately aware of the wealth of tennis activity, with courts frequently in use beside the entry road. The tennis courts and bowling green take up a large part of the north-east corner of the ground, just as tennis, together with cricket, dominates the atmosphere during the summer. *(Courtesy Cheam Sports Club)*

Tennis courts, Cheam Sports Club, 12 April 2003. Modern floodlit courts mean that tennis is a truly all-year-round game, with the most (fool)hardy playing during a frozen evening having dusted the frost from the baseline first. Tennis was the second sport to be incorporated into Cheam Sports Club, in April 1920 under its secretary F. Stanley Thomas. The section grew rapidly, having 200 members and nine courts by 1922, and two hard courts, sited where the present all weather courts are, by 1927. The tennis section maintains its social tradition with players of all ages, standards and abilities playing on any of the grass and hard courts available. They even encourage the next generation with special tennis classes during school holidays. *(George Hobbs)*

Cheam Bowls Club, 1930s. The bowls club was founded in 1932 and it is tempting to think that the founder members are depicted in this photograph. Sadly no names now survive for the players seen here. The first green was sited on ground previously rented by the tennis section; the old tea hut (see page 110) was moved from near the drive and placed between the tennis courts and bowling green and both sports used it as a shelter. Even so the bowling green was small and members had to wait until 1945 before the repositioning of the adjacent tennis courts allowed them to extend their green to full size. The railway embankment is clearly visible in the background of the picture and, up to 2 July 1938 when steam passenger services were replaced by electric on the line (occasional steam freight continued until the 1960s), bowls matches could be obscured several times an hour by drifting smoke and cinders from passing engines. *(Courtesy Cheam Sports Club)*

Cheam Bowls Club, 1960s. Bowls is certainly the most relaxing sport to be played at Peaches Close, or at least that's the impression it gives. The bowls section is extraordinary in many ways when compared with some of the other sections in the sports club. Bowling continues all year round, indoors and out, in team and individual events, and the members even built their own clubhouse. Early in the 1960s the section extended membership to ladies; late in the same decade water was laid on to the bowls pavilion. It is not known whether the two events were connected. . . . Left to right in this picture are C. Milne, Stan Street (who was vice-president of Cheam Sports Club in 1964) and Harold D'eath. It is not certain whether Messrs Street and D'eath are ensuring the wood is being delivered correctly or debating who should help their colleague back up! *(Courtesy Cheam Sports Club)*

Cheam Hockey Team, 1926. Back row, left to right: E.T. Williamson, D.E. Comer, R. Leins, H.E. King, E.H.C. Cooper (umpire). Middle row: L.A. Balls, E.G. Porter, J.D. Crosthwaite, E.J. Henderson, W.L. Shorting. Front row: R.C.H. Toye, D.J. Brannan. Hockey was the third sport to be incorporated into the Cheam Sports Club. The section was formed in 1921 under Mr and Mrs Percival Thomas, secretaries of the men's and women's sections respectively. This is one of the earliest known photographs of Cheam Hockey Club and shows how far both the sport and how it is played has come on in the last eighty years. (Courtesy Cheam Sports Club)

Hockey match, Cheam Sports Club, 1980. Anyone driving past the club during the winter months up until the mid-1990s would have seen the hockey section playing on any one of the four grass pitches they had surrounding the main cricket square. While they still use the clubhouse as the base for pre- and post-match celebrations (and the number of League titles they have won gives an indication of the amount of celebrating they have been forced to endure), they are now obliged to play all their matches on Astroturf which it isn't possible to install at Peaches Close. It's a far cry from 1940 when members of the hockey section pulled a heavy roller from Cheam recreation ground, along Malden Road and through the village – a distance of over a mile – to help flatten pitches damaged by bombs. The light building to the left in the background is more recent and houses the squash courts. After several years of work and fundraising the courts were opened on 11 February 1979 and squash became part of the club. (Courtesy Cheam Sports Club)

Cheam Sports Club 'pavilion', early 1920s. Accommodation was spartan in the early days and an ex-army tin hut served as bar, canteen and tea room. No hot showers in those days either! In almost a century the club has grown to need three pavilions and has recently even had to hire Portakabins to provide enough room for players to change in. Even in the twenty-first century pre-fabricated buildings still seem to be the answer. *(Courtesy Cheam Sports Club)*

Pavilion, Cheam Sports Club, 24 May 2003. Opened in 2001, the new pavilion provides a sideways view of the cricket square and overlooks the main football pitch. The photograph is taken from the site of the old pavilion (see page 97), which is now an overflow car park. And so we've come full circle, 139 years after Cheam Sports Club was founded by local traders Messrs Noakes (brewer), Chadband (tailor), Napper (baker), Corbett (horse-drawn cab owner) and others. One item of subtle interest: by 1876 Edward Boniface had acquired the brewery in Cheam from John Noakes and it is as a brewer that he is named in the deeds to the club's land. The current sponsor of the League in which Cheam Cricket Club plays is a brewery, so maybe things don't change after all. *(George Hobbs)*

6

And Now for Something Completely Different . . .

Aviary, Nonsuch Park, *c.* 1970. Anthony Watson was an associate of Lord Lumley who made him rector of Cheam in 1581. Watson became bishop of Chichester in 1596 but continued to live in Cheam and probably built the older part of Cheam rectory. He also left a detailed description of Nonsuch Palace which remains an invaluable source of information to archaeologists and historians today. One of the things Watson described was a 'wire-fenced enclosure crowded with pheasants and partridges from across the sea'. The palace aviary also included pelicans, peacocks and guinea fowl. The modern aviary is much smaller, but in much the same tradition. *(Ron Taylor, Cheam Camera Club)*

W e've already established that Cheam has a listed building a foot wide and over a mile long, but there are many more oddities around the area for the curious to enjoy and which refuse to be docketed neatly. 'Miscellaneous' is always the fullest pigeon-hole. . . .

Talking about pigeons, West Cheam Manor House (see page 7), might have been demolished soon after 1796, but its octagonal brick pigeon house with ogee and lead-trimmed tiled roof survived until about 1902. It stood where Park Road is now and today would probably have been converted into a small house. It was huge. Pigeons were a source of food and the manor house must have had a very large larder.

Cheam House, which stood between The Broadway and Park Lane, was let at the beginning of the twentieth century. As it was empty at the outbreak of the First World War it was used to house German prisoners of war until the Armistice was signed. Cheam was apparently home to German prisoners of war during the Second World War too, and the pre-fabs which once stood in Cuddington Way were supposed to have been built by them. Perhaps that's why an amateur film company filmed there. Cuddington Way had its fair share of evacuees and must have been safer than Cheam Park. Cheam Park House was so badly damaged by bombs that it had to be demolished after the war. Its curved driveway still exists, however, and strollers in the park probably wonder why the path deviates oddly at that point.

During the war much of Cheam Park was dug up either to grow food or for air-raid shelters, but Nonsuch Mansion House escaped too much bomb damage. The house is now in the care of the local authority and occasionally opened to the public. Visitors may care to look out for a verse hidden round the eaves of the entrance hall: 'Welcome for all, greetings for many, love for a few. / Farewell goes out sighing, by these laws, true / Friendship is expressed.' Very few illustrations of Nonsuch Palace remain (see page 30) but Cheam has one of its own inside the Lumley Chapel. The sides of the first Lady Lumley's tomb show her three children kneeling in a stylised interior which is said to be that of the palace.

Did you know that Cheam has two or possibly even three plague pits? One is in St Dunstan's churchyard, south-east of the Lumley chapel, a second is rumoured to be under the men's fifteenth tee on Cuddington Golf Course, and a third may exist to the west of Cuddington Way. Other subterranean finds include a fourteenth-century kiln excavated from Park Side (see introduction to chapter 4) which is now in the Science Museum in Kensington, Roman coins on Howell Hill, and a Saxon burial found when digging a bunker on Cuddington Golf Course.

For a settlement which traces its history back hundreds of years the area seems to be remarkably lacking in resident ghosts. Even Anne Boleyn's Walk is a misnomer. It's not as though Cheam lacked incident. Cheam Hall once stood on the south side of Tate Road, where the cricket pitch is now. It was the home of Mrs Eliza Dutton, who is buried in Cheam churchyard. The inscription on her tomb states: 'Eliza Dutton, who was murthered the 13th July, 1687, by her neighbour whilst endeavouring to make peace between him and his wife' (*sic*). The flowery verse which follows ends with a rather unchristian sentiment: 'May that curs'd hand forget itself to feed / That made its benefactor thus to bleed.' It seems fairly obvious that everyone knew who had perpetrated the deed and so perhaps the shade of Eliza Dutton had no need to walk.

Another murder connected with Cheam, although only indirectly, was that of the poet and playwright Christopher Marlowe. He was killed in Deptford Strand, London, on 13 May 1593 and his inquest would normally have been overseen by the local coroner. However, Elizabeth I and her court were staying at Nonsuch at the time and special legal provisions applied to 'The Verge', the name given to the area within a 12-mile radius of wherever the court happened to be at the time. The coroner of the queen's household, William Danby, was therefore called on to officiate. Some would argue that Marlowe was the Anthony Blount of his day and was killed deliberately by the government of the time. There may be some truth behind the supposition. Measurement of miles was still flexible in the sixteenth century but even so Nonsuch was probably some 16 miles away. The rules governing The Verge did not apply. So how did Danby know he was needed?

Today anyone seeking help would probably just pick up their mobile phone, but in the days when a whistle was the sole aid a constable had there was a police box at the corner of Cuddington Way. Some such boxes were mini police stations and included telephone, first-aid kit, bench desk, stool, fire extinguisher and dustpan and brush to keep the place tidy. Perhaps squeezing that lot in gave someone the idea for the tardis.

Detection has never been the sole prerogative of the police force, and at one time a very famous firm of private investigators, Carratu, was based in North Cheam. They shared McMillan House with a number of small firms who were amazed to see their sometime colleagues appear on television after a successful raid on a warehouse in Essex. No one in the building had had any idea, until that time, what the firm did.

Residents in rural areas have always had to make their own entertainment, and Cheam was no exception. The women gossiped, the men went to one of the many pubs (nothing changes!) and the children, well, they went ice-skating. Early in the twentieth century the water table was still high enough for Bony Hole to fill with water (see page 16), particularly in winter. When it froze the locals would skate on their own ice-rink. Archery and beekeeping, leisure activities from an even earlier age, are still practised in Cheam. The Nonsuch Bowmen practise regularly in the area and several local residents have hives in their back gardens.

Memorials celebrating the Millennium sprouted up all over the country, and Cheam has at least two – with different dates on them. The village sign on the south-east corner of the crossroads (see page 1) is dated 2001. The statue of the risen Christ over the entrance to St Christopher's Roman Catholic Church is accompanied by a plaque which says: 'this statue of the risen Christ was blessed on 26 November 1999 to launch the celebration of the great holy jubilee of the year 2000 AD.' The argument continues.

Calling the following photographs 'oddities' is as untrue as it is unkind, but they do show a side of Cheam not perhaps revealed in earlier chapters. And, of course, they don't 'fit' nicely anywhere else. . . .

Peacock, aviary, Nonsuch Park, 13 May 1990. Peacocks are natives of East Asia, but were imported into Britain in the fourteenth century to add ornament to stately homes. They also made a tasty and exotic addition to the table as they were roasted and served in their own plumage. In spite of being such big birds they fly well and often roost in trees: in India, if the birds don't perch high enough, tigers sometimes seize their huge tails and haul them down for a quick snack. Peacocks tend to be noisy and bad-tempered, which may be why Nonsuch Park no longer keeps them. Today the aviary contains nothing more spectacular than chickens, but their feathers are pretty enough and children still enjoy watching them. *(George Hobbs)*

Fox, South Cheam back garden, June 2001. Urban foxes are opportunists and hundreds of them have colonised the various open spaces. Watching them is easy – just keep still. Foxes see movement extremely well, but sacrifice for this gift the ability to see stationary things clearly: a fox can easily mistake a still figure for a tree or post. Occasionally Cheam has been host to even more exotic wildlife. During the 1980s a wallaby was found hopping happily around Cuddington Golf Course. It disappeared and nobody seems to know what happened to it. Perhaps the nineteenth tee was particularly popular that day! *(Author's collection)*

No. 25 Malden Road, *c.* 1936. The child is
Dennis Turner who lived with his mother
and maternal grandparents, Mr and Mrs
Muggeridge, in no. 25. The house was
one of a row of ten on the brow of the
hill. Nos 25–27 and 31–34 were as
shown, but 28–30 were smaller and built
of wood. Mr Muggeridge was a platelayer
on the railway and he, his wife and
daughter 'did' for wealthy people on the
other side of the tracks. Mr and Mrs
Muggeridge were also caretakers at
Ambleside School (see page 64) for a time.
(Dennis Turner)

No. 25 Malden Road, 9 March 2003.
A short terraced row of three single-storey
bungalows now stands on the site;
no. 25 is in the middle. Each is designed
as a small, self-contained dwelling for the
elderly. The block stands much closer to
the road than the house in the original
photograph, but the Prince of Wales pub
opposite and the Scout hut next door to
the south both still survive.
(George Hobbs)

No. 61 Holmewood Road decorated for Victory in Europe (VE) day in 1945. Mr and Mrs Reed stand near the front door and their daughter Marjory is near the garage. The Reeds' son, Dennis, was in the air-sea rescue which might explain the white ensign on the right. *(Muriel Reed)*

No. 61 Holmewood Road, 20 March 2003. The house has changed remarkably little. The chimney has sprouted a television aerial, the porch has been enclosed and a new garage door has been fitted. Even the double glazing has been carefully chosen to fit with the character of the house. The biggest change is in the maturity of the surrounding foliage. *(George Hobbs)*

Well Head, Spring Close Lane, 21 April 2003. The neat brick hut was built to house the pumping equipment needed for the well head. There are not many areas which can boast their own water supply, but much of Cheam's water comes from wells in the village. A bad water supply makes a community very vulnerable, so good security is essential to avoid tampering. For this reason reservoirs that store the purified water before distribution are often not marked on maps. Shame about the graffiti. Why *do* people do it? *(George Hobbs)*

Drilling for water, Spring Close Lane, 1992. Water companies make huge efforts to ensure that we have clean, fresh water on tap whenever we want. A doodle scribbled in 1971 by W.D. Smith expresses fulsome recognition: 'Water from my taps doth flow / To bring life's vital drink. / The Sutton District Water Co. / Deserves my thanks I think.' Disruption to the water supply is rare, whatever the weather. What many in Cheam don't realise is that much of our water is pumped to treatment works from boreholes such as this one being drilled in Spring Close Lane. *(Ron Taylor, Cheam Camera Club)*

Probably around the junction of Church Hill Road and Senhouse Road, North Cheam, 1953. The Elizabethan costumes indicate that the fair was to celebrate the coronation of the second Queen Elizabeth. The packets held bath salts with the same scent as the flower pictured. Left to right: Graham ?, Josephine Morgan, Margaret Harris (now Margaret Holland), Barbara Nightingale, Pat Wakeford, Brian Warner. *(Margaret Holland)*

The Palace Crystals, Cheam Village Fair, 26 May 2003. Cheerleading began in Britain in 1982, with the Carshalton Cheerleaders being formed just over a decade later in 1993. The group is divided into Palace Crystals, Cheer Magic and Pom Crazy, depending on age. The Palace Crystals are the senior team or 'cheer' and were adopted as official cheerleaders by a well-known football team. Apart from regular visits to Selhurst Park they make guest appearances at local and national events and have won several major competitions. Ninety-seven per cent of all cheerleaders are female, but there have been several famous men who have joined a cheer, including Dwight D. Eisenhower and Kirk Douglas. Like it or not, you have to admire the stamina and athletic prowess of the group. *(George Hobbs)*

Knife-sharpener, Stoughton Avenue, 1971. One of the London street cries was 'Knives to Grind' so this knife-sharpener is one of the last of a long tradition. The spelling error may well be deliberate – after all he is 'at the sharp end'. Note the solid rubber tyres on his portable grindstone, and the cover for the equipment carefully folded and stowed over the axle away from the grit of the road. Apart from the introduction of a motor, the barrow has changed very little for well over a century. Most travelling street traders of this sort have been put out of business by our throwaway society, but, with more and more businesses moving out of town on to trading estates, and good services becoming rarer, there may well be growing a niche which the smaller entrepreneur can fill. *(Ron Taylor, Cheam Camera Club)*

The Wheelie Bin Cleaning Company, Cheam Park, 26 May 2003. Perhaps street services are not dead after all but have merely changed with the times. The Wheelie Bin Cleaning Company does exactly what it says on the van. One of their representatives calls every fortnight to brush, clean, deodorise, line and label wheelie bins before returning them to the door. On the right in the picture is Ian Bundle, franchisee and regional manager. *(George Hobbs)*

Coalman, Stoughton Avenue, *c.* 1972. It was the first delivery of the day, so he was not covered in grime. Today far fewer of us have coal fires and health and safety regulations wouldn't permit anyone to hump this sort of weight about anyway. Coalmen used to work on very much the same terms as some milkmen do today and contracted to buy in certain goods from a central distributor and then sell them on for what profit they could make. Used to lifting heavy weights and with their own robust transport, many coalmen also moonlighted as hauliers. *(Ron Taylor, Cheam Camera Club)*

Chimney sweep, Onslow Avenue, 20 June 2003. Coalmen might be a dying breed but chimney sweeps are still essential, whatever sort of fuel you use. The National Association of Chimney Sweeps recommends that chimneys in use should be swept at least once a year to ensure that deposits don't build up and hamper the efficient use of whatever appliance or fire is using the flue. Standard equipment has improved, however, since the days when small boys were pushed up chimneys. In addition to brushes, vacuum and breathing equipment is now standard. As the Vac Sweep, Colin Parkinson, demonstrates, the sweep often leaves the room cleaner than when he found it. *(George Hobbs)*

North Cheam, 16 October 1987. Derek Poulter is a keen amateur radio operator whose aerial mast usually rises to 50 ft. Built to withstand high winds, the mast, which is bedded in concrete and bolted to the house, nevertheless ended up a tangle of expensive tubular aluminium. Following the hurricane, insurance claims totalled £1,500 million across the South East, with as many as one in six households making a claim. *(Sue Poulter)*

North Cheam, 5 April 2003. Even for an expert, repairing the mast was no easy matter and took several months. As much as 20 ft of special tubular aluminium went into its construction, together with replacement aerials. It certainly makes an impressive addition to the house. Incidentally, eagle-eyed readers will notice that the number plate of Derek's car (G3WHK) reflects his amateur radio call sign. *(George Hobbs)*

Hurricane damage to a builder's yard, corner of Elmbrook Road, October 1987. Not a good advertisement for the building firm, but with winds gusting in excess of 100 mph there is perhaps some excuse. Surrey recorded the lowest ever barometric reading for October in the early hours of Friday 16 October 1987. No wonder the hurricane hit. *(Ron Taylor, Cheam Camera Club)*

The back of TMS motor-parts shop, corner of Elmbrook Road, 21 April 2003. Except for some necessary clearing up and repair very little of the scene has changed. The cars are newer and a few traffic-calming measures have been introduced. They obviously never did get round to replacing the wall. *(George Hobbs)*

Hurricane damage, Gander Green Lane, October 1987. Cheam has many attractive roads lined with foliage, but they became one giant log pile as trees were toppled like skittles. This silver birch may have been uprooted, but firm grounding was no guarantee of security as sturdy trunks were snapped like matchsticks in the punishing wind. Emergency services struggled to get through and residents were without power, telephone and, in some cases, water. Incredibly, in spite of the devastation the worst of the storm passed Cheam to the south. *(Ron Taylor, Cheam Camera Club)*

Gander Green Lane, 21 April 2003. An ordinary suburban road with nothing now to show that anything unusual had happened. Of course there is the new tree, hiding behind the lamppost on the left. . . . *(George Hobbs)*

Cheam and Worcester Park Day Centre Float, Cheam Fair, Cheam Park, *c.* 1988. Until recently Cheam Fair included a procession of decorated floats which paraded around the village. Tableaux depicting anything from historical events to famous stories were a traditional part of any carnival. Such pageants combined pre-television entertainment, advertising and a handy means of fundraising. With the exponential growth in interactive multimedia, few now seem to bother. *(Ron Taylor, Cheam Camera Club)*

Wax and Wain, Cheam Fair, Cheam Park, 26 May 2003. If audiences are less tolerant of amateur – in its most pejorative sense of 'not very well done' – offerings, good live entertainment is still a draw. Billed as a comedy trampoline duo, Wax and Wain managed the difficult task of being both entertaining and highly skilled. Entertainment may have changed from the 'Elizabethan' sellers of bath salts (see pages 118–19) and certainly from the hare coursing of Henry VIII's time (see page 25), but if it harms nobody does it matter? I wonder if they'll let me have a go next year? *(George Hobbs)*

ACKNOWLEDGEMENTS

Without the support, suggestions, help and photographic skills of my husband, George Hobbs, this book would not have been possible. I am also grateful to my editors at Sutton Publishing, Simon Fletcher and Michelle Tilling. Simon responded to questions about what to do and how to do it – some of them probably fairly inane and a few positively irritating – with unfailing promptness, tact and patience, while Michelle efficiently transformed a pile of photographs into a series of attractive pages.

Every effort has been made to locate all the copyright holders and obtain their permission to use the photographic material included in this book. If there has been any error or omission in crediting the correct individuals or organisations the author can only apologise.

I am indebted to many organisations for their willingness to help with photographic material for this book. They include: Capital Transport Publishing, Cheam Camera Club, Cheam Sports Club, Churches Conservation Trust, Cloud 9, Cuddington Croft Primary School, Cuddington Golf Club, Dairy Crest, Felicity Hat Hire, G. Hana Photography Ltd, London's Transport Museum, Nursing Times, Oxfam, R. Durtnell & Sons Ltd, St Andrew's United Reformed Church, St Anthony's Hospital (www.stanthonys.org.uk), St Paul's Church Centre, Howell Hill, Sutton and Cheam Radio Society (www.scrs.org.uk) and The Sainsbury Archive.

I should also like to thank the many individuals who kindly provided help, information, cups of tea, sympathy and assistance with worrying. Many of them also allowed their photographs and other material to be reproduced. They include: Lucy Barr, Joan Barratt, Noel Bibby (archivist for St Andrew's URC), Gary Bishop, Gary Corcoran (who wrote many of the captions for Chapter 5), Philip Cook (marketing manager at St Anthony's Hospital), Alan Cross, Lilian Curd, Toni Frei, Caroline Furey (assistant archivist for J. Sainsbury), Margaret Holland, Fr Russell Lawson, Bob Malcolm, Angela Masters, David Morgan (archivist for Cheam Sports Club), Colin Parkinson, Muriel Reed, Derek and Sue Poulter (who put a great deal of effort into checking the facts regarding amateur radio), Hugh Robertson (curator of photographs at London's Transport Museum), Mr B. Steptoe, David Stevens (archivist for J. Sainsbury), Ron Taylor, Christine Thomas, Bob Tillin and Dennis Turner.

BIBLIOGRAPHY

Much of the information for the captions in this book has been provided by the people who have loaned the photographs, but some has, of necessity, been derived from other documentation. The author acknowledges with gratitude the debt she owes to the following publications:

Anon, *Church Guide*, St Paul's Church Centre, Howell Hill, 1992

Anon, *The Sutton District Water Company 1863–1963*, Sutton and Cheam Water Company Ltd, 1963

Burgess, Frank, *Cheam, Belmont and Worcester Park*, Phillimore, 1993

Burgess, Frank, *Cheam Village past and present*, London Borough of Sutton Leisure Services, 1991

Davison, Mark and Currie, Ian, *Surrey in the Hurricane*, Froglets Publications Ltd, 1988

Dent, John, *The Quest for Nonsuch*, London Borough of Sutton Libraries and Arts Services, 1981

Jackson, Patricia, *Whitehall and Cheam Village*, London Borough of Sutton Leisure Services, undated

Leach, Robert, *History of St Mary's Church, Cuddington*, St Mary's Parochial Church Council, 1995.

Marshall, C.J., *History of Cheam and Sutton*, Cryer's Library, 1936.

Marshall, Charles J. and Roberts-West, Maud, *A History of the Village of Cheam with Local Guide*, Dudley G. Rix, undated

Mitchell, Vic and Smith, Keith, *London Suburban Railway: West Croydon to Epsom*, Middleton Press, 1992

M.S.B. and N.H.B., *St. Andrew's, Cheam*, 2nd edn, St Andrew's United Reform Church, Cheam, 1990

Peel, Edward, *Cheam School from 1645*, The Thornhill Press, 1974

Proctor, Patricia E., *Cheam Sports Club: Diamond Jubilee, 1920–80*, Cheam Sports Club, 1980

Thorns, J. Gilbert, *Sir Gilbert Cheyham (Doubly a Knight): A Romance of Nonsuch Palace*, Arthur H Stockwell Ltd, undated

Western, Edward, *The Daughters of the Cross at St Anthony's*, St Anthony's Hospital, 1995